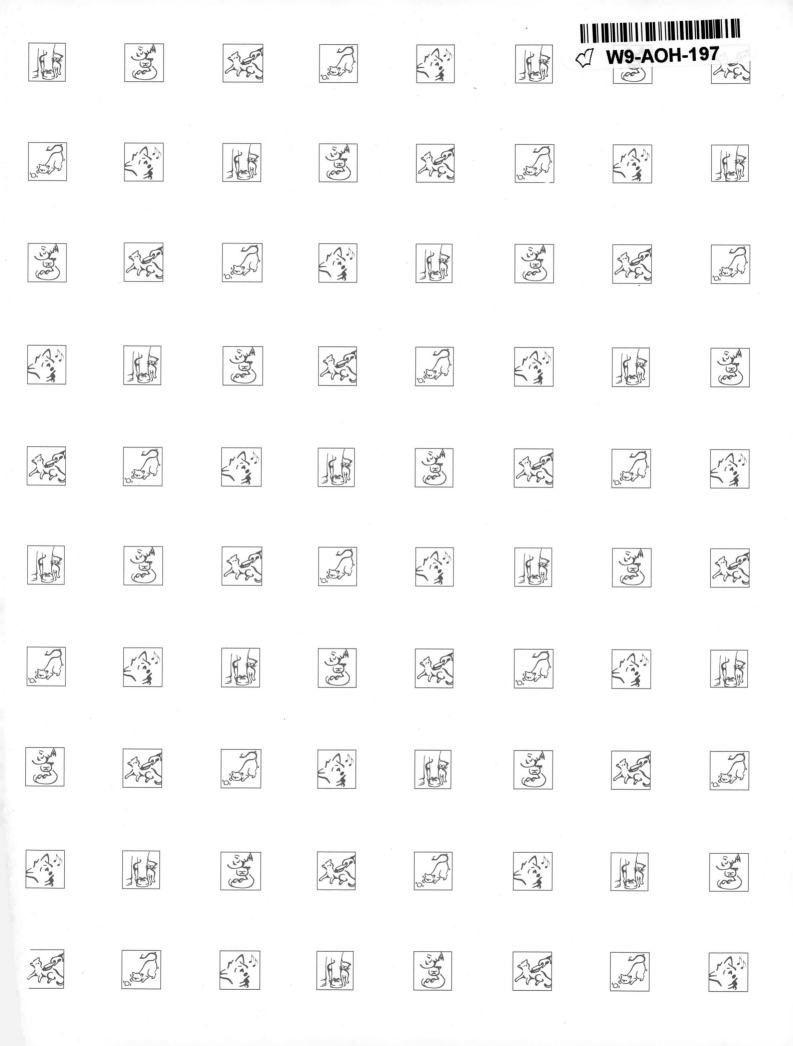

CATS

An Owner's Guide

CATS
An Owner's Guide

Carla Atkins

BARNES & NOBLE

NEW YORK

Photo Credits
The publisher would like to thank the following people for their help in the preparation of this book: Kerry Ryan, editorial assistant; Phoebe Tak-Yin Wong, graphic design assistant; Samantha Marland; Marc, Chloe, and Lottie van Grieken (and Fudge and Squinky); Orlaith and Naoimh Hughes; Lydia and Jane Tarran (and Honey, Rosie, Jessie, and Bramble); Iona and Cara Tavendale; Nick James (and Ben); Max and Winifred Robertson.

All photographs in the book are © Nikki L. Fesak unless otherwise listed by page number below:

© **2002 Arttoday.com, Inc.:** 8, 9b, 10 (both), 11 (all), 12, 13t&br, 124t&b, 127tr&bl, 140tl, 147bl, 155br, 175bl, 179 (all except tl&cr), 180 (cl, cr & bl), 183tr&c, 184tl, 186tr, 187br, 189tl&cl, 190tl, 191b, 192t&bl, 194cr, 198cr&br, 199bl, 200tl&cl, 201cl, 202 (all except tl&br), 206cr, 217t&c, 219tl&cl, 234br, 235 (all except c), 236tc&bl, 243 (all); **Bibliothèque Nationale, Paris:** 9tr; © **Comstock, Inc.:** 1, 5, 6tl, 115l&r, 122 (tr, cl & cr), 123tl, 126tl, 128 (3rd row r & bc), 130 (all except cr), 131tl, 132bl, 135br, 141tl&bl, 143br, 145b (both), 146tr, 147tl, 148tr, 149c, 160tl, 162br, 174b (far right), 175tr, 178r (all), 181tr, 187tl&tr, 192cr, 198bl, 200bl, 201c (far left), 203tl, 212tr, 217br, 224tl, 226t, 228c, 233tr, 234tl&bl, 239tl&tr, 240tl, 241br, 244br, 245tr, 246 both); © **Corbis Corporation:** 114tr, 119br, 127br; © **Photodisc, Inc.:** 116bl&br, 147cr; **Max & Winifred Robertson, Loismhor:** 173r (all), 208b (all), 209b (all), 231 (all cats); © **Alan Robinson:** 3, 6 (all cats except 3rd row c & br), 7 (tl,tr&bc), 112 (all cats except 2nd row c), 113 (all cats), 128 (all cats except bc), 129 (tl,tr&bc), 142 (all cats except tr & 2nd row c), 162 (tl, tr, 3rd row l & bc), 196t (l&r) & 3rd row (l&r), 224 (all cats), 225 (all cats except br), 238 (all except tc & 2nd row c), 239 (tc, bc & br), 249 (both), 254b&r, 255b, 256; © **Charles J. Ziga:** 135cr, 247l.

All photographs between pages 14–111 are © Alan Robinson except the following: © **Nikki L. Fesak:** 14 (2nd row c & bc), 17t, 19tr, 22tr&cl, 23 (both), 24b (both), 27b, 28t, 29t&c, 35 (all), 36tr, 60bl, 62c, 64t, 68b, 73bl&tl, 104t, 106t, 110tl; © **Charles J. Ziga:** 66 (both).

EDITOR: Sara Hunt
MANAGING EDITOR: Karen Fitzpatrick
ART AND PRODUCTION EDITOR: Deborah Hayes
PHOTOGRAPHY: Nikki L. Fesak and Alan Robinson
ASSOCIATE EDITOR: M. Jane Taylor

ISBN-13: 978-0-7607-8236-1
ISBN-10: 0-7607-8236-9

Library of Congress Cataloging-in-Publication Data:
Atkins, Carla.
    Cats: an owner's guide / Carla Atkins.
        p. cm.
    Includes bibliographical references and index.
        ISBN 0-7607-8236-9
1. Cats. I. Title.

SF442.A84 2003
636.8–dc22   2003066287

Printed and bound in China

1 3 5 7 9 10 8 6 4 2

Key to Icons

 Cats of this breed tend to be affectionate toward their owner.

 These cats are usually well-suited to households with children.

 Considerable grooming is required to maintain the condition of the coat.

 These cats are usually playful.

 Cats of this breed are highly vocal.

CONTENTS

Introduction

Cats in History

Our most popular pet has a distinguished lineage that goes back to prehistoric times. Its ancestors appeared after the age of the dinosaurs, when mammals became divided into two basic groups: flesh-eaters and plant-eaters. The short-legged, fish-eating Creodants, which had clawed feet, were long believed to be the forerunners of today's cats, but recent evidence points to the Miacids, which emerged some 60 million years ago as the Creodants were dying off.

Originally, the Miacids were insect-eaters that ranged in size from today's weasel to a large dog. They had short legs and long bodies and frequented primeval forests. These animals are now regarded as the original ancestors of wildcats, lynxes, and cheetahs, as they eventually developed forty sharp teeth, including the four large molars or premolars in the

Feline Facts

🐾 The cult of Bastet emerged about 1500 B.C. at the town of Bast, northeast of Cairo, and grew rapidly into a national phenomenon. Great temples were built in honor of the goddess, and countless cats were mummified as sacred companions to the dead. Her worship was associated not only with fertility, but with music, pleasure, and dance, which resulted in orgiastic rituals that lasted for days. Later, this would be a factor in the persecution and hatred of cats in Christian Europe during the Middle Ages.

upper and lower jaws that are adapted to hold and tear flesh with a shearing action.

From the Miacids evolved groups of feline carnivorous species including the *Felidae*. Of these, it was the fleet-footed felids that survived, including the ancestors of the roaring cats (for example, lions and tigers), the cheetah, and numerous small members of the family *Felis*, including the domestic cat.

Evidence of early domesticated cats appeared during an archaeological dig on the island of Cyprus in 1983, which suggested that the cat was living alongside humans as long ago as 8,000 B.C. However, the role of the domestic cat in ancient Egypt more than 3,000 years ago is far more fully documented in the artwork of this high civilization. Here the cat served as household companion, pest controller in the granaries, hunting companion for birds in the Nile marshlands, and most famously, as the goddess of fertility, Bastet.

🐾 *One of the domestic cat's many wild relatives, the serval* (Felis serval) *shares much of its genetic makeup. Native to Africa, this handsome, swift, graceful creature typically measures about two feet at shoulder height.*

🐾 *A cat as witch's familiar appears in this etching from Francisco de Goya's (1746–1828) satirical series entitled* Los Caprichos.

From Goddess to Demon

In medieval Britain and Europe, under the aegis of the Roman Catholic Church, cats became identified with "pagan" (pre-Christian) cultures and were considered minions, or even incarnations, of Satan, especially in their supposed role as witches' familiars. Countless innocent women were persecuted, even burned alive, as witches, and their unfortunate cats—especially black cats—suffered the same fate.

Gray cats were also targeted for persecution. Readers may recall the reference to "Graymalkin" in Shakespeare's *Macbeth* (1603), in which one of the three witches calls out, "I come, Graymalkin," implying that the cat was one of her familiars.

Remnants of this cruel age have come down to us in the form of superstition. For example, in America, having a black cat cross one's path is a harbinger of bad luck. And Halloween (originally the major Witches' Sabbath of Samhain), coincident with the Christian feast of All Hallows Eve, is inevitably identified with the image of a menacing black cat.

Feline Facts

🐾 Artist Leonardo da Vinci (1452–1519) was far ahead of his time in his admiration of cats. Declaring that "Even the smallest feline is a work of art," he made detailed sketches of the subject in a page that is now held in the Royal Library at Windsor, England. The collections of the British Museum include a number of mummified cats from Bast (later Bubastis).

This negative attitude persisted into the eighteenth century, when Francois-Augustin Paradis de Moncrif was savagely ridiculed for his book *Les Chats* (1727), the first major work on the subject, and had to withdraw it from publication. However, by 1790, we find an early illustration of a domestic tabby seated in a window embrasure in Thomas Bewick's *General History of Quadrupeds*.

🐾 *Left: It is difficult to see why creatures like this cute kitten acquired negative associations.*

The Domestic Cat Comes to the New World

Some eight to twelve million years ago, when Eurasia became detached from the Western Hemisphere, the descendants of the ocelotlike *Pseudailarus* were among the most successful mammals to colonize the Earth. Lions once ranged from parts of South America through North America, Asia, Africa, and Europe. Wildcats of African descent, the ancestors of today's housecats, were found throughout Europe and Asia. When they became domesticated, they were taken to new parts of the world aboard ships to control rodents. Farmers valued them for the same purpose. Thus we have the familiar "ship's cat" and "barn cat," which arrived in the Americas with post-Columbian settlers from many European lands.

The ancestors of these cats was probably marked with black bars on a ground of tawny and white, which served as camouflage among the grasses and shrubbery where they ranged. To this day, the tabby pattern is the commonest among non-pedigree cats—and seen in many pedigreed breeds as well. It still serves its purpose when the animal is hunting. In fact, the name "Tabby" is almost synonymous with "cat." (It is also suggested that the

familiar diminutive "Puss" originated from the name of the cat goddess Bastet, also called Pasht.)

Cat colonists of the New World were hard workers, like their human companions. They routed mice and rats from barns, warehouses, and granaries, often slept and hunted outdoors, and were expected to earn their keep. Prolific breeders, they soon became more and more widespread, as immigrants moved from the East Coast to the West, and from Middle America north into the present-day Southwest.

🐾 *Above, the ubiquitous tabby, whose coat pattern provided camouflage in the wild. At left, a modern-day ship's cat enjoys luxurious quarters.*

The Cat's Prestige on the Ascendant

During the mid-eighteenth century, a profeline movement originated in France and began to change the popular image of the cat as treacherous, wily, and hypocritical. Important writers like the poet Charles Baudelaire, author of *The Flowers of Evil,* praised the cat's sensuality, while novelist Alexandre Dumas (who kept a small zoo), was described as "defense lawyer of cats of all the world."

The gifted Colette, a nineteenth-century cabaret dancer and writer, cherished her cats and included them in many of her autobiographical works. She also had her photograph taken in a feline pose modeled on the Sphinx.

Shakespeare had written affectionately of cats in *The Merchant of Venice* and *Henry V,* and later British cat-lovers followed in his footsteps. T.S. Eliot, Rudyard Kipling, poet Algernon Charles Swinburne, and novelist George Eliot all had a deep appreciation for the feline species and eulogized their cats and others in their works.

American writers, too, began to eulogize the cat in their works. Edgar Allan Poe, in his short story

> *"Stately, kindly lordly friend*
> *Condescend*
> *Here to sit by me, and turn*
> *Glorious eyes that smile and burn,*
> *Golden eyes, love's lustrous meed,*
> *On the golden page I read."*
>
> —from Swinburne's *To a Cat*

Above: Cats have populated Eastern monasteries for many centuries to control mice. Perhaps this habitat has contributed to their serene image. Artists, as well as literary scholars, have frequently depicted feline subjects (left).

"The Black Cat," described the cat he called Pluto as "My favorite pet and playmate. I alone fed him, and he attended me wherever I went about the house." Ernest Hemingway was known for his love of cats, as was essayist, novelist, and humorist Mark Twain, who wrote that "If a man could be crossed with the cat, it would improve man, but it would deteriorate the cat."

Cat Shows and the Cat Fancy

Harrison Weir was the first to organize a cat show, at London's Crystal Palace in 1871. The RSPCA came into being here, and was followed by the creation of the American Cat Fancy Association in New York City. The first all-American cat show took place in 1895 at the original Madison Square Garden. From these beginnings, "the fancy" spread to many other countries, and today hundreds of cat shows are held every year.

England set the standard for the important pedigree document (a term first used for horses of pure blood), which includes the name of the animal, breed, color, sex, date of birth, and complete list of its genealogy.

Into the Twenty-first Century

Since the 1980s, cats have outnumbered dogs as the Number One pet in America. One reason for this is the cat's adaptability to our increasingly urban way of life. A cat can be kept in a small apartment and leash-trained, if desired, to expose it to the outdoors safely. It can also be kept indoors exclusively. In the suburbs, one can build a sturdy enclosure in the yard where cats can enjoy fresh air and sunshine without the risk of getting lost, attacked, or infested with parasites. Even a sunny windowsill with a view of activities and wildlife in the yard will content most cats.

In rural areas, and in many cities as well, cats often become feral as a result of abandonment and uncontrolled breeding. Many humane people and organizations seek to alleviate this feline overpopulation problem with spay/neuter programs, volunteer veterinary care, and shelters that adhere to a no-kill policy, promoting adoption where possible and providing lifelong care where a permanent home is not an option. As people become more aware of the responsibilities of pet ownership and the commitment it requires, hopefully, this situation will improve.

Recent research and firsthand experience have shown that keeping a cat provides a valuable source of companionship and measurably reduces the stress of our hectic contemporary lifestyle. In the widespread absence of extended family groups, a strong sense of community, and other support systems that have eroded over time, a companion animal has become even more important to young people, the elderly, and those who are working ever-longer hours just to stay even with fluctuating economies. In many cases, a cat is our closest contact with the renewal provided by nature herself.

> *"The cat of the slums and alleys, starved, outcast, harried...still displays the self-reliant watchfulness which man has never taught it to lay aside"*
> —Saki

The Purpose of This Book

It is hoped that this comprehensive guide to finding and caring for the feline friend who is exactly right for your circumstances will add a new dimension to your life. If you have already experienced the joys of cat ownership, you will find this the ultimate source for cat lovers, covering, as it does, nutrition, grooming, exercise and play, home safety, basic training, veterinary care, and a host of other subjects.

The full-color, step-by-step photographs are an invaluable asset to the text, and the historical highlights provide fascinating insights into the evolution of the feline race. Perhaps most importantly, this guidebook will strengthen the bond of love between you and your cat and help you to appreciate even more the wonderful warmth, humor, and devotion that your companion animal brings to your relationship.

Adopting a kitten or cat brings many years of companionship, fun, and a few surprises, too. In turn, pet ownership involves responsibilities, which this book outlines in detail.

I
Cat Breeds and Types

Long-Haired Breeds

The lovely long-haired breeds have become increasingly numerous and attractive since the first Persian cat was shown at London's Crystal Palace more than a century ago. Breeders have perseveringly selected for coat characteristics and optimum personality traits within their breeds, both long established and newly emerged, like the Balinese. The result is an ever-wider range of colors, patterns, and coat types. Personalities, too, differ among the breeds, although each cat is individual. The Persian, for example, while it may look aloof, is known to be loving, companionable, and quiet. The Maine Coon, "made in the USA," is both adaptable and active, while the silky Angora is busy, curious, and loyal. The long-haired nonpedigree may be just as handsome and good-tempered as his regal relatives, although his coat, too, will be higher-maintenance than that of the short-haired breeds. The examples that follow give some idea of the beauty and diversity of these appealing animals.

Persian Longhair

We may imagine that the dusty camel caravans of the ancient Spice Road that ran westward from Persia and Iran sometimes carried, along with jewels and exotic spices, a rare and beautiful long-haired cat. It was called Persian for its supposed country of origin, but similar cats have been discovered in hieroglyphic references dating back to 1684 B.C. We cannot be sure how long domestic cats of this type have been bred, but in the early twenty-first century, they are the most popular of all the pedigrees.

🐾 Who could resist the wide-eyed expression of this fluffy, orange-eyed white Persian? With its long, flowing, snow-white coat, this is a cat of sheer beauty. It is easy to see why Persians are the most popular breed in the world.

In the United States, some 30,656 Persians were registered with CFA in 1999, and another 765 with TICA. Their open, pansylike faces and calm, gentle dispositions, added to the flowing beauty of their "coats of many colors," have made them Eastern stars wherever they are shown. TICA chairperson Rebecca Brown, in an interview with *Cats U.S.A.* (2001 Annual), states that: "Whenever you see a Persian, you should think round and square. They have a round head, ears, and eyes. Their cobby body (that's the square) is supported by thick legs, and

their fluffy tails tend to be short, ideally in proportion to their cobby frames." The following description of a show-quality white Persian was written for *Cat Fancy* (June 2002) by Lorraine Shelton in the article "Rhapsody in White":

🐾 Solid or "self" colors: These include whites (above), which can be blue-eyed, copper-eyed, and odd-eyed, as well as creams, blacks (see detail, left), blues, reds, lilacs, and chocolate, all of which have brilliant copper eyes.

"Spectators gasped when the judge placed her on the table. Her immaculate, snowy white coat billowed around her like an elegant gown. A truly unforgettable Persian of ethereal beauty, Grand Champion Wishes Lyric exemplifies the ultimate white cat."

😺 Parti-Color: Among this small but striking division is the red-and-black tortoiseshell, with variants including blue-cream (shown below, right), lilac-cream, and chocolate-cream tortoiseshell. The pattern consists of the two colors splotched randomly over the cat, and often a mark down the nose and under the chin, called a blaze. Eyes should be copper in color.

😺 *The aristocratic expression on the tortie point above may seem snooty, but Persians are affectionate and gentle companions. Far left: red Persian variations include the red shaded cameo, which has red-tipped fur.*

We have all seen images of such feline aristocrats in movies and cat-food commercials (think of the finicky spokescat for Fancy Feast, named Gimel), but the fact is that Persians come in nearly every color and pattern imaginable.

😺 Calico and Bicolors: This division comprises calicos—white cats with red and black splotches— as well as the lilac, blue, and chocolate calicos and any of the solid, smoke, tortoiseshell, shaded, and tabby colors with the addition of white. Preferably, these cats have brilliant copper- to orange-colored eyes, like the red-white Bicolor shown at right.

The Persian's jaws are broad and powerful, and its neck is very short and thick. Round, brilliant eyes must conform to the coat color, and the feet are well rounded, preferably with long tufts of fur between the toes, which are carried close, four in front and five behind.

Behavior: Persian cats are notable for their calm, gentle, and affectionate ways. They respond to petting with appealing chirps and murmurs, and quickly become accustomed to the extensive daily grooming and monthly bathing needed to keep their beautiful coats free of mats. Since the Persian sheds year-round, daily combing and brushing are essential, and show cats must always be kept indoors.

🐾 *Persians can be prone to showing off—or maybe it's just their natural beauty that gives us that impression.*

🐾 Golden: The Shaded Golden, with green to hazel eyes, is also in high favor with cat owners and show judges alike. Golden Persians have a luxurious apricot- or golden-colored undercoat with darker tipping along the back and on the head and tail.

Appearance: The ideal Persian is a medium to large, heavily boned, and well-balanced cat with a sweet expression and softly rounded lines. The chest is broad and deep, with a very full ruff, and the rump and shoulders are of equal width. The head is broad and well rounded, having a domed forehead with no vertical ridges. The tufted ears are small and round-tipped, set well apart and low on the head. The nose is short and snub, and there is a definite horizontal indentation between the eyes, called the break.

Temperament: Much of the Persian's charm is in its gentle, loving qualities as a companion and its beautiful, expressive eyes. This cat usually exudes contentment and thrives in a quiet household. It seems to love admiration, and often "poses" for hours draped on a chair or windowsill. These qualities contribute to its excellence as a show cat.

🐾 *The attractive, distinctive appearance of the Golden Persian is due to the shading on the individual hairs (see fur detail, left).*

😺 Tabby: This division consists of cream tabby, brown tabby (right), blue tabby, red tabby, silver tabby, chocolate tabby, lilac tabby, cameo tabby, and torbie, in any of the four tabby patterns: classic, ticked, mackerel, and spotted. Except for the silver tabby, eye color must be copper.

😺 *The brown tabby (below) was very popular in Britain in Victorian times, when the Brown Persian Cat Society was founded.*

Special Characteristics: The Persian (known as the Longhair in Britain) is considered a separate breed by each color there and may have a slightly different standard. This cat has lost the ability to hunt and fend for itself, so feral Persians are, fortunately, almost unknown.

Origins: The original Persian's flowing coat was probably a mutation that developed in the face of a cold climate. Ever since the breed became known in Europe during the 1600s, its beauty has inspired breeders to perfect and diversify its coat.

😺 *Above: detail of the brown tabby's coat.*

😺 Shaded and Smoke: This comprises shaded cameos (white cats with red tipping) and shaded versions of all the solid colors, all of which should have copper eyes. The pewter (right) features a white coat that is tipped with black to create a pewter effect. The lovely Smoke Persian has a snowy white undercoat and often a luxurious white ruff. This is essentially a white cat so heavily shaded on its outer hair with one of the following colors that it resembles a solid-colored cat: cream, black, blue, cameo, lilac, chocolate, and tortoiseshell. Most Smokes have copper eyes.

Chinchilla Longhair

As mentioned earlier, in the UK, each Longhair color has a slightly different standard for head and body type, while the U.S. requires that all Persians must compete to the same exacting standard.

🐾 The Chinchilla is very similar to the Silver Shaded Persian, in terms of its facial shape, body, and shading. However, the color is paler in the Chinchilla, which appears almost white.

Behavior: Like other types of Persian, the Chinchilla is sweet-natured, adaptable, and loving. It enjoys being fussed over, which is an asset, because its long, beautiful coat requires daily grooming.

🐾 *This long-haired, silky cat is a docile creature that will shower you with love and affection. Be prepared to do the same for a Chinchilla, too, as these cats don't have the most independent of feline personalities.*

Appearance: The differences between the Chinchilla and the Persian (Longhair) Silver Shaded are minor—in fact, kittens of both types occur in the same litter. The Chinchilla has long, silky, thick white hair that is delicately tipped. The tipping is significantly less pronounced than in the Silver Shaded, giving the Chinchilla a lighter, almost pure-white, overall appearance.

Temperament: The Chinchilla has a quiet, melodic voice and differs from other Persians mainly in having a body type that is less stout than the average. It has a placid disposition and does best in a relatively quiet home.

Special Characteristics: The elegant, even fairylike, appearance of the Chinchilla has made it popular in television commercials like those for Fancy Feast cat food and in films, where it features as a pampered princess.

🐾 *If you have infants, boisterous toddlers, or young children in your household, the Chinchilla may not be the pet for you—at least, not until the children have grown a few years older. This is typically a sensitive, gentle animal that likes a reasonably quiet life and is easily overwhelmed by too much of the rough and tumble of children's games.*

Origins: The earliest Chinchilla of which we have a record was named Silver Lambkin and attracted great attention at London's cat shows during the late nineteenth century.

🐾 The Chinchilla Silver is pure white with delicate black tipping on the ends of the hairs, brick-red nose leather, and blue-green eyes.

Himalayan Longhair

🐾 *This seal point Himalayan has the typical medium-to-large body set on short, strong legs.*

The beautiful, blue-eyed Himalayan originated in 1924 by crossings among Siamese, Birman, and Persian cats. In Britain, Himalayans are identified as Persians/Longhairs in various colorpoints rather than as a separate breed. The name is derived from the Himalayan rabbit, which is similar in color. As with the Siamese, all varieties must have a well-marked mask, ears, legs, paws, and tail.

Many U.S. breeders produce and show both Himalayans and Persians, which are considered by some associations as separate breeds, by others as Himalayan Persians.

🐾 A tortie point Himalayan (detail above) sports a thick, silky coat, with no wooliness, and a luxuriant frill.

Appearance: The Himalayan body type is like that of the Persian: solid with short, strong legs, a short neck, and a broad, rounded head. The sapphire-blue eyes are round and the Himalayan has plump cheeks, a short nose, small and wide-set ears, and a flowing coat that is more than four inches long, with an abundant ruff. The tail is straight and not as thickly haired as the body. Recognized colorpoints include seal, blue, chocolate, lilac, red, tortie, blue-cream, and lynx (markings of tabby design in various colors).

Behavior: This is an affectionate, gentle cat that does not fight with other cats and shows few of the more flamboyant traits of its Siamese forebears. Quick to learn, the Himalayan can be leash-trained for outings and has a soft, musical voice.

Special Characteristics: Male Himalayans reach sexual maturity at eighteen months, which is considerably later than the females. Most litters number only two or three kittens, which are born entirely white, with short hair; markings are not usually established until the age of six months.

🐾 *This group of Himalayan colorpoint kittens shows them at their most appealing. As they grow, they will develop affectionate dependence on their owners.*

🐾 It is thought that Himalayans were the first deliberate hybridization of two breeds: the Persian and the Siamese. As you can see, these kittens have the fluffy Persian coat plus the exotic colorpoint markings of the Siamese. However, their blue eyes are less vivid in color than those of their Siamese forebears.

Temperament: An easygoing personality makes this cat a favorite with the whole family, although its sweetness of character may predispose it to bond more closely with one member or with a single owner.

Origins: The Himalayan was originally bred to transfer the pointed pattern of the Siamese to the Persian type, which has been accomplished successfully over the past eighty years.

Birman

The beautiful Birman's origins are shrouded in mystery, but it has long been identified as the sacred cat of Burma (now Myanmar), a companion to its Buddhist monks, perhaps as long ago as the golden age of Lao-Tsun, Grand Lama of Buddhism. As in Egypt, the Birman was venerated as a divinity. The characteristic long, silky coat of the contemporary Birman results from crossbreeding with the Persian.

and have white boots on all four feet (see also the short-haired American variety called the Snowshoe on page 85). There are a number of colorpoints recognized for championship showing.

Appearance: The Birman is a long, large, stocky cat with a well-rounded head and full cheeks. It has an appealing expression, enhanced by its somewhat rounded muzzle and well-defined chin. The deep-blue eyes are also round, and the medium-sized ears are set well apart on the head.

🐾 Chocolate Point: Mask, ears, tail, and legs are chestnut brown, except for the pure white paws.

Reportedly, early in the twentieth century, a pair of Birman cats was secretly shipped to France from their native land. The male died during the long voyage, but the female, Sita, arrived safely and was found to be pregnant. This small foundation stock was enough to establish the Birman in the West, beginning with its recognition as a separate breed by France in 1925.

Birman kittens are born with a light, solid-colored coat; their markings appear a few months-later. All Birmans are blue-eyed

🐾 Seal Point: A pale golden body with white mittens and gauntlets, dark brown points, and blue eyes.

Temperament: The Birman is gentle by nature, with a very pleasing personality. It is especially good around children and generally enjoys robust health.

Special Characteristics: In an interview by Ellen Kanner in *Cats U.S.A.* (2001 Annual), breeders James and Paula Jo Watson of Bitaheaven Cattery in Conway, Arkansas, discussed the traits that have made them dedicated to the breed. "They're very personable, very loving, very people oriented," says Paula Jo, who spends all of her time caring for the couple's "all-stars" in the Watsons' large home. Queens who are about to give birth are placed in birthing cages that line the bedroom wall and monitored around the clock until they deliver their kittens.

Five stud rooms, each with a window, cat tree, bed, and litter box, have been included in the converted two-car garage, which has its

Heavy-boned legs of medium length are in proportion to the body, and the paws are large, round, and white. The paw pads are pink, or pink spotted with the point color, and the medium-length tail is quite bushy. Daily combing and brushing are mandatory to keep the Birman's luxuriant coat looking its best. Note that the breed is slow to mature, undergoing some awkward, adolescent-type stages before reaching its full potential.

🐾 Lilac Point (above and right): Mask, ears, tail, and legs are pearl gray. Nose leather is lavender-pink and paw pads are pink. The strongly built body is a beautiful light, creamy magnolia color.

Behavior: This is an intelligent, soft-voiced, well-behaved cat that is a pleasure to have around. Independent by nature, it enjoys moderate activity, including walks in the garden. It tends to pine when its owner is away.

Feline Facts

🐾 More recently developed Birmans in the colors of red point, tortie point, and lynx point are gaining wider popularity among breeders, but are still in the process of achieving universal acceptance for championship showing.

🐾 Blue Point: Similar to the seal point, but with gray-blue mask, ears, tail, and legs. The body is white with a bluish tint. Eyes in this variety should be a deep blue color.

own separate heat and air systems. Apart from this, the cats have the run of the house. And after a decade of breeding, the Watsons have developed an instinct for which kittens in a litter may have show potential.

A cat may have the right looks, but the wrong personality for shows, being too shy or becoming bored with the constant travel and life in the limelight. In this case, its needs are honored and it is retired to the cattery.

One of the Watsons' "top cats" is Bitaheaven Vandal, who became a Grand Champion National Winner in 2000. The CFA rated two-year-old Vandal the eleventh-best cat in the country, only the second Birman ever to make a national win. But after a year of tireless campaigning, Vandal was growing restless with the show circuit and was allowed to retire. "He's still running the house," says Paula Jo, "and sleeps in the bed with us." It takes a very special cat to inspire this kind of devotion.

Origins: As mentioned above, the Birman was not recogized as a separate breed until 1925, when the French cat registry bestowed this status upon it. Britain waited until 1966 to extend recognition, and the United States followed suit during the following year.

🐾 Blue Tortie Tabby: The delicate-colored points of this ideal Birman combine tortie and tabby markings with china-blue eyes for an almost ethereal appearance. Legend says that the Birman acquired its beautiful white feet when the ancestral cat rested his paws on the white hair of his dying master.

Ragdoll

The early development of this breed was controlled by the original breeder by franchise. Its ancestry involved several nonpedigreed cats, and its origins were embroiled in controversy. The Ragdoll is a color-pointed cat that comes in the traditional point colors—lilac, blue, seal, and chocolate—in each of three patterns: colorpoint, mitted, and bicolor. At this writing, the CFA accepts only the bicolor for championship showing. The cat was introduced in Britain in 1981 and gained recognition there two years later.

These appealing cats are delicate-looking but sturdy animals. Their gentle nature helps make them easy to train.

Bicolors (below, both) have white fur on their underparts and an inverted "V" in the mask, extending to the outer edge of the eyes.

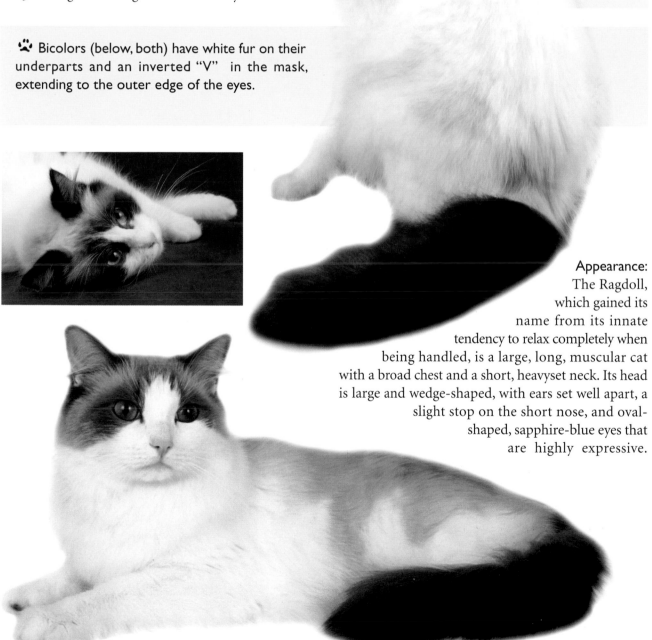

Appearance: The Ragdoll, which gained its name from its innate tendency to relax completely when being handled, is a large, long, muscular cat with a broad chest and a short, heavyset neck. Its head is large and wedge-shaped, with ears set well apart, a slight stop on the short nose, and oval-shaped, sapphire-blue eyes that are highly expressive.

The fur on the front legs is short and thick, while that on the hind legs is longer and thicker. The Ragdoll's coat is plush and silky and must be combed daily with a wide-toothed comb and then brushed gently with a long-bristled brush. The breed standard calls for tufted paws with pad colors that harmonize with the coat.

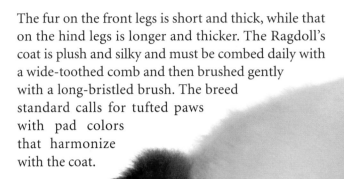

🐾 *These blue tabbies (below and right, below) show the sweet, loving expression and the blue eyes typical of this breed.*

Behavior: This gentle, good-natured cat is eager to please and rarely destructive or aggressive toward people and other animals.

Temperament: The Ragdoll quickly becomes attached to its owner and has a loving and adaptable nature, as its name suggests. It is docile, intelligent, and usually good with children.

Feline Facts

🐾 California breeder Ann Baker bred the first Ragdolls in the 1960s and went on to form her own breed association. Eventually, the Ragdoll acquired championship status with major registries.

Special Characteristics: Ragdoll kittens begin to develop their characteristic points at about one week of age. Males are larger and heavier than females.

🐾 *Red and Cream Ragdolls have subtle, beautiful colorpoints. The Cream is the dilute of the Red Ragdoll.*

Origins: The founding mother of this breed was a random-bred white longhair named Josephine who was injured in a car accident in California during the 1960s. As a feral cat, her previous litters had been wild and incapable of being handled, but when she recovered from her injuries, she delivered a litter that impressed people with their gentleness and sociability. At this point, the founding breeder, Ann Baker, acquired as many of Josephine's kittens as she could and began to breed them for docility of temperament. The unscientific theory that the accident somehow accounted for the kittens' gentle dispositions persists to this day, as does the fallacious idea that the Ragdoll cat is incapable of feeling pain.

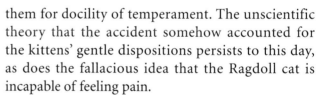

🐾 Both Red and Cream Ragdolls are becoming increasingly popular.

Siberian Forest Cat

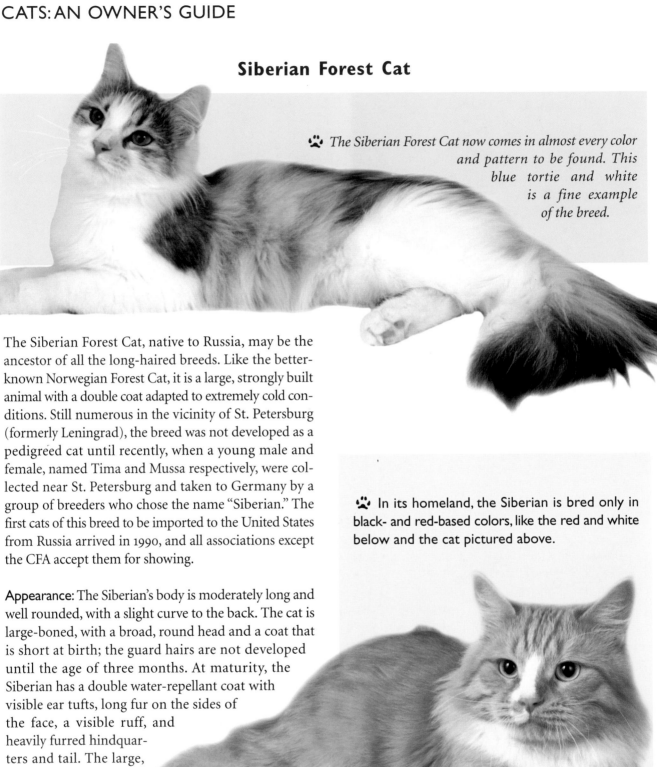

🐾 *The Siberian Forest Cat now comes in almost every color and pattern to be found. This blue tortie and white is a fine example of the breed.*

The Siberian Forest Cat, native to Russia, may be the ancestor of all the long-haired breeds. Like the better-known Norwegian Forest Cat, it is a large, strongly built animal with a double coat adapted to extremely cold conditions. Still numerous in the vicinity of St. Petersburg (formerly Leningrad), the breed was not developed as a pedigreed cat until recently, when a young male and female, named Tima and Mussa respectively, were collected near St. Petersburg and taken to Germany by a group of breeders who chose the name "Siberian." The first cats of this breed to be imported to the United States from Russia arrived in 1990, and all associations except the CFA accept them for showing.

🐾 In its homeland, the Siberian is bred only in black- and red-based colors, like the red and white below and the cat pictured above.

Appearance: The Siberian's body is moderately long and well rounded, with a slight curve to the back. The cat is large-boned, with a broad, round head and a coat that is short at birth; the guard hairs are not developed until the age of three months. At maturity, the Siberian has a double water-repellant coat with visible ear tufts, long fur on the sides of the face, a visible ruff, and heavily furred hindquarters and tail. The large, round eyes are usually golden-green, and the coat may be any pattern or color except colorpoint, solid chocolate, or solid lilac. Brown tabby is the most common coat color, perhaps because of this cat's wild forebears.

Behavior: Still rare in the United States, the Siberian is gaining popularity as an active, intelligent cat that adapts to family life quite readily and can tolerate cool climates.

Temperament: While its appearance is robust and muscular, the Siberian has a gentle, winning disposition that makes it a loving companion. It resembles the Persians in being vocally quiet rather than talkative.

Special Characteristics: Like the Norwegian Forest Cat, the Siberian sheds its heavy, glossy winter coat in spring and summer and should be groomed regularly to prevent the formation of hair balls.

Feline Facts

🐾 The Siberian Forest Cat was little known as a breed until the 1950s, when it was recognized by registries in its homeland, including the A-U-Russian Cat Club.

Origins: Russia has taken a growing interest in its native cat, and there is now a birth registry for Siberian Forest Cats at the Kotofej Cat Club in St. Petersburg. The cat was first exhibited in the United States at the International Cat Show in New York City in 1991.

🐾 *Left: A beautiful black tortie with a luxuriant coat of many colors.*

33

Norwegian Forest Cat

This handsome breed resembles the Maine Coon in many respects, but its dense, furry coat is shed in the spring so that it appears to be a short-haired cat, except for the tail plume and lynxlike tufts on the ears. Native to central Norway, it may have inspired such legends as that of the giant cats that pulled the chariot of Freya, goddess of beauty, love, fertility, and—sometimes—war. This gift of the Norse gods was little known beyond its native land until a dedicated group of Norwegian breeders resolved to establish a program aimed at saving the *Norsk Skogkatt* from extinction in 1975.

Right: A red and white Norwegian Forest Cat displays the thick coat and plumelike tail that distinguish this handsome, sturdy breed. Below, an appealing study in point colors: red silver tabby, tortie, and tortie smoke kittens.

Appearance: As might be expected of a breed that evolved near the Arctic Circle, the Norwegian Forest Cat is large, robust, and endowed by nature with a two-layer coat designed to keep it warm and to shed water. The silky outer coat gives the cat a full ruff and britches during the winter months, while the tail is heavily feathered year-round. Heavily muscled hind legs make this cat a strong climber. The head forms an equilateral triangle with widely set, pointed ears and almond-shaped eyes that slant upward. Brown tabby and white is the most popular color, but the "Wegie" comes in a wide variety of colors and patterns.

🐾 *This handsome cat, with its shaded red and cream colors, has a characteristically thick, luxuriant winter coat. The expressive eyes of this breed, which resembles the Maine Coon, are almond-shaped.*

Behavior: This cat adapts to almost any kind of household, and it is not shy about demanding attention. If its owner is preoccupied with paperwork, it is quite capable of jumping onto her desk and knocking papers to the floor.

🐾 *Two views of a tortie smoke and white Norwegian Forest Cat.*

35

Special Characteristics: The long winter coat does not demand high maintenance. The Norwegian Forest Cat should be combed at least once a week, and during the spring the abundant undercoat sheds in a matter of days. An occasional bath will help keep the coat clean and glossy.

🐾 *Opposite, top: An elegant blue smoke Norwegian Forest Cat at rest. In addition to tortie and blue, there are several other smoke coats seen in this breed, including cameo and golden smoke.*

"Baloo was at the Madison Square Garden Cat Show in March. She's a Norwegian Forest Cat. She was just hanging out on the chair, very laid back. I think it's remarkable for a cat to act that way at a cat show. I'd be a wreck."
—Robin Schwartz

Temperament: The Norwegian Forest Cat enjoys the presence of people, other pets, and children, if they are not rough and boisterous. It is generally mild tempered and patient, but it needs a companion if left for long periods. It continues to mature until almost five years of age.

🐾 *Blue tabby and white (above and below) is an increasingly popular color form of the "Wegie."*

🐾 Left: A beautiful calico with kitten. Detail (right) and below: These appealing kittens are growing into their two-layer coats, which are water repellant and not affected by rain or snow—perfect for their native Scandinavian habitat, where winters can be severe.

Origins: When this native breed came close to extinction after World War II, the Norwegian Forest Cat Club, *Norsk Skogkattring*, was formed under the leadership of Carl-Frederick Nordane. He presented the breed to the Federation Internationale Feline (FIFe) in Paris in 1976, and the club won recognition as an accepted breed the following year. It is now recognized by all of the North American associations.

Turkish Van

This handsome cat is indigenous to the wintry Lake Van region of Turkey, and this accounts for the seasonal nature of its coat, which is much thicker during the cold months than in the summer. It is especially unusual in that it loves to swim and readily enters the water. It became known in Europe when two English photographers, Laura Lushington and Sonia Halliday, returned from a vacation to Turkey in 1955 with a pair of these cats and subsequently imported several more. The cats' white kittens with auburn markings on the head and tail resulted in the breed now known as the Turkish Van.

In the West, auburn and cream Turkish Vans like these are the most familiar color forms, with eye color a distinguishing feature. Unfortunately, deafness is a problem that may appear in blue-eyed cats. Moreover, when an odd-eyed cat has one blue eye, hereditary deafness may affect the ear on the same side as that eye.

Appearance: This is a solidly built cat with a broad chest and hips and powerful legs. Males are larger than females, but both have the delicate bone structure of the Turkish Angora. The head is wedge-shaped, with a neat, rounded muzzle, a rounded chin, and a downward curve to the nose. Walnut-shaped eyes are large and expressive and are usually blue, amber, or an odd-eyed combination of these two colors; all three of the eye-color types are rimmed with pink. The tufted ears turn slightly outward, and the coat is unique in pattern. In fact, auburn color over more than twenty percent of the cat is subject to penalty in judging, although localized "thumbprints" of auburn on the body are allowable. The legs are medium length and wide-set, with back legs longer than the front. The rounded feet have tufted toes and the tail is a brush or plume of medium length.

Feline Facts

In its homeland, the ideal Van is all white, like the Turkish Angora, with one blue and one amber eye. Auburn markings are considered undesirable—despite their attractive appearance.

Behavior: Once considered an aggressive animal, the Turkish Van has been modified by more than a half century of breeding and is now considered a highly desirable and amusing pet, especially in its proclivity for taking to the water.

A graceful odd-eyed Turkish Van with characteristic markings.

Temperament: This lively cat enjoys protected access to the outdoors and is very affectionate. It tends to bond most closely with one or two family members and has a melodious voice that is quite distinctive.

Special Characteristics: In the absence of a thick, woolly undercoat, these long-haired cats are relatively easy to groom. They should be combed daily, especially in the early summer, when they shed their thick coats. The two most widely recognized colors are cream (cream markings contrasting with the chalk-white coat, with a vertical white blaze separating the colored areas of fur on the head) and auburn, where the auburn areas on the head are confined to the area above the eyes.

Origins: The Turkish Van was registered in Britain in 1969 and in North America in 1985.

Top Tips from Readers of *Cat Fancy,* 2002

- If a chubby cat needs additional exercise, locate the food dish at the top or bottom of the stairs so she can climb for extra physical activity.

  —Marjorie Marlowe, Clinton, Iowa

- Keep miniblind strings out of cats' reach so they don't become tangled in them.

  —Christine Salo, Sandwich, Massachusetts

- Place rubber shelf liners under the cat food bowl to prevent your cat from pushing it across the floor.

  —Kathy Cain, Urbana, Illinois

- Spread the cat food in one layer on a pie pan to prevent cats from eating too fast and to reduce regurgitation.

  —Tonya Rodriguez, Elyria, Ohio

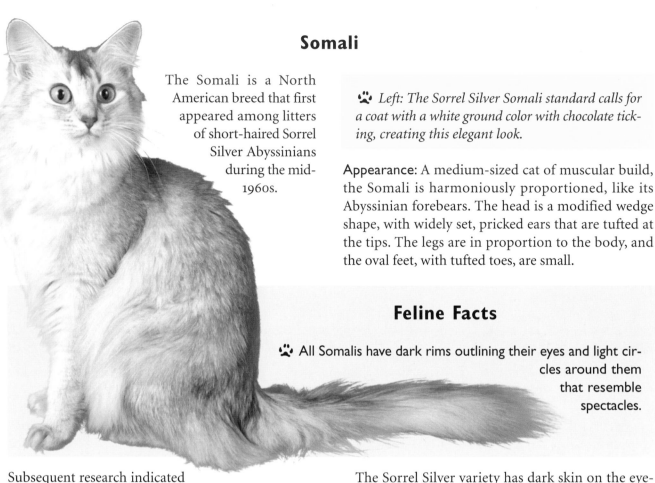

Somali

The Somali is a North American breed that first appeared among litters of short-haired Sorrel Silver Abyssinians during the mid-1960s.

🐾 *Left: The Sorrel Silver Somali standard calls for a coat with a white ground color with chocolate ticking, creating this elegant look.*

Appearance: A medium-sized cat of muscular build, the Somali is harmoniously proportioned, like its Abyssinian forebears. The head is a modified wedge shape, with widely set, pricked ears that are tufted at the tips. The legs are in proportion to the body, and the oval feet, with tufted toes, are small.

Feline Facts

🐾 All Somalis have dark rims outlining their eyes and light circles around them that resemble spectacles.

Subsequent research indicated that some bloodlines of the Abyssinian had, in fact, carried the recessive gene for long hair through several generations. Thus the Somali was named for the African country that borders Ethiopia (formerly called Abyssinia) because of its relationship to the short-haired cat. The new breed was officially presented at European shows in 1977 and granted championship status by the CFA the following year.

🐾 *Right: A blue tortie smoke Somali shows its sleek elegance.*

The Sorrel Silver variety has dark skin on the eyelids, with a lighter circle around the eyes; almond-shaped, hazel-colored eyes; and an apricot undercoat over white hair with the characteristic ticking—in this case, chocolate, which also appears on the tips of the ears and tail. The Sorrel Somali—a rich copper color—has soft, fine, double-coated fur, with a brushy tail and short hair on the head. The richly colored Ruddy Somali has a golden-brown coat with black ticking most prominent on the spine and tail. Ideally, it has a full ruff and britches of longer fur on the legs and underparts.

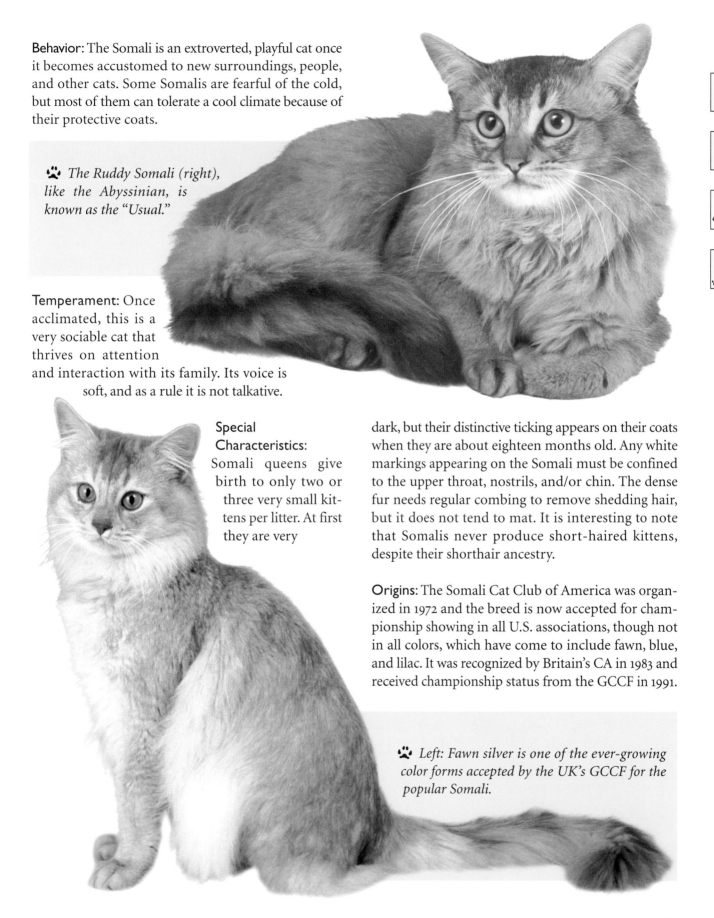

Behavior: The Somali is an extroverted, playful cat once it becomes accustomed to new surroundings, people, and other cats. Some Somalis are fearful of the cold, but most of them can tolerate a cool climate because of their protective coats.

🐾 *The Ruddy Somali (right), like the Abyssinian, is known as the "Usual."*

Temperament: Once acclimated, this is a very sociable cat that thrives on attention and interaction with its family. Its voice is soft, and as a rule it is not talkative.

Special Characteristics: Somali queens give birth to only two or three very small kittens per litter. At first they are very dark, but their distinctive ticking appears on their coats when they are about eighteen months old. Any white markings appearing on the Somali must be confined to the upper throat, nostrils, and/or chin. The dense fur needs regular combing to remove shedding hair, but it does not tend to mat. It is interesting to note that Somalis never produce short-haired kittens, despite their shorthair ancestry.

Origins: The Somali Cat Club of America was organized in 1972 and the breed is now accepted for championship showing in all U.S. associations, though not in all colors, which have come to include fawn, blue, and lilac. It was recognized by Britain's CA in 1983 and received championship status from the GCCF in 1991.

🐾 *Left: Fawn silver is one of the ever-growing color forms accepted by the UK's GCCF for the popular Somali.*

41

Angora

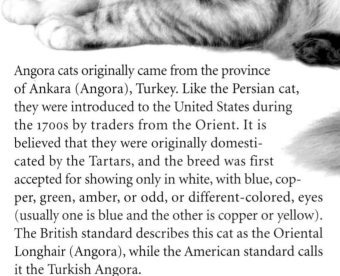

Angora cats originally came from the province of Ankara (Angora), Turkey. Like the Persian cat, they were introduced to the United States during the 1700s by traders from the Orient. It is believed that they were originally domesticated by the Tartars, and the breed was first accepted for showing only in white, with blue, copper, green, amber, or odd, or different-colored, eyes (usually one is blue and the other is copper or yellow). The British standard describes this cat as the Oriental Longhair (Angora), while the American standard calls it the Turkish Angora.

Appearance: This is a beautifully balanced cat with an alert, intelligent expression. The body type is the same as the Siamese, Balinese, and Oriental Shorthair— long and svelte.

A chocolate silver shaded tortie Angora (above); at left, the green-eyed black Angora.

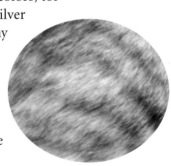

The coat is fine and silky in texture, and the tail is a long, elegant plume. In Britain, the colors and patterns are widely diverse: self colors, torties, smokes (having a silver undercoat), tabbies of any pattern, and shaded. All of the above colors have green eyes, while the traditional all-white Angora may be green-, blue-, or odd-eyed (one green and one blue).

"Who can believe that there is no soul behind those luminous eyes!"

—Theophile Gautier

Origins: The true Angora was slowly becoming extinct, being replaced by the Persian/Longhair. Strenuous efforts to maintain pure bloodlines have been established by Turkey's Ankara Zoo, which breeds only white Angoras.

Behavior: The Angora is considered an excellent pet, having a lively interest in its surroundings but cherishing its serenity. It is well suited to a single owner.

"Wonderful, wonderful is our life, and that of our companions! That there should be such a thing as a brute animal, not human! That it should attain to a sort of our society with our race! Think of cats, for instance; they are neither Chinese nor Tartars, they neither go to school nor read the Testament. Yet how near they come to doing so, how much they are like us who do."
—Henry David Thoreau

🐾 *The gorgeous cinnamon Angora (above) has a warmly colored brown coat, with no white hairs (see fur detail, left); the paw pads are pink or brown. The cat below is the caramel shaded variety.*

Temperament: Primarily an indoor cat, the Angora is often portrayed as reclining on a cushion in a sphinxlike pose, at ease, but friendly and engaging in manner.

Special Characteristics: There is no undercoat, so grooming is simpler than it is with other breeds. Daily combing with a medium-toothed comb will remove dead hair and prevent matting, especially when the winter coat is being shed during the spring. Note that white Angoras with blue eyes are occasionally born deaf.

Turkish Angora

"Like a graceful vase, a cat, even when motionless, seems to flow."
—George Will

Appearance: The Turkish Angora has a long slender body with fine bone sructure and a wedge-shaped head set on a long, slim neck. Lithe and well balanced, this cat has a long, somewhat pointed nose and large, almond-shaped eyes that slant upward slightly. The eyes can be of any color, although white cats with odd eyes are valued highly because of their rarity. In white specimens, the nose leather should be pink; in other colors, it should harmonize with the coat color. Ears are large, upright, tufted, and set high on the head.

This cat has long, sturdy legs and small paws, preferably with tufting between the toes. The white Turkish Angora has pink paw pads, while those of other colors are in keeping with the coat color. The long, plumed tail tapers from a wide base to a narrow tip. The

As discussed on pages 42–3, Angoras, the beautiful, long-haired cats from Turkey that first reached Europe during the sixteenth century, enjoyed increasing acclaim as they spread from France and Italy to other parts of the Continent. However, by the time the first cat shows were held in the nineteenth century, the Persian was quickly gaining preference over the Angora, which fell into rapid decline as a breed. Outside of their country of origin, Angora bloodlines had been much diluted by crossings with Persians. After World War II, the breed was recognized by the CFA in the early 1970s, but only in the original color— white. This changed in 1978, when many new colors (see below) were developed, most recently using cats imported from Turkey's Ankara Zoo.

🐾 *White is the traditional color of this breed. Eye color varies from odd-eyed to blue- and amber-eyed.*

fur is fine, dense, and silky and appears to shimmer as the cat moves; there is no undercoat. A long ruff and britches are desirable, and coat colors range from blue, black, blue smoke, silver tabby, red tabby, and the classic white to bicolors of many kinds. In fact, all colors and patterns are now registered with the exception of colorpoint, solid lilac, and chocolate.

Behavior: The Turkish Angora is gentle, nonboisterous, and well suited to an indoor life because of its rather sedentary nature.

Temperament: These cats receive high marks for their intelligence, friendliness, and charming ways and have been described as excellent pets.

Special Characteristics: Because of the lack of undercoat, this long-haired breed is relatively easy to care for. Its coat should be combed regularly, especially when the winter coat is being shed, to avoid hair balls. Note that the coat is not fully developed until the cat reaches the age of about two years. Mating with other breeds is not authorized.

🐾 *This graceful red tabby shows off the fine bone structure and silky coat that are typical of the breed.*

🐾 *The head of the Turkish Angora is wedge-shaped, with a relatively narrow muzzle. This blue tortie and white shows typically rounded eyes and widely spaced, medium-sized, pointed ears.*

Origins: A strong impetus to the Turkish Angora's revival in the United States was given during the 1960s when breeder Liesa Grant imported a pair from the Ankara Zoo named Yildiz (Star) and Yildizcik (Starlet). (The Turkish breeding program produces only white cats, which are considered the national cat of Turkey.)

Feline Facts

🐾 Charles Darwin and other naturalists of his time may have believed that the Turkish Angora had evolved from the wild Pallas's cat—a theory that has been disproved.

Balinese

nose. The tail tapers to a fine point, where the hair is longest. Legs are long and slim, with the hind legs longer than the forelegs. The Balinese has small, oval paws whose pad colors harmonize with the coat color. As with the Siamese, the ears are noticeably large and pointed, rising from a wide base to accentuate the wedge shape of the head.

🐾 *Left and bottom of page: The elegant cream Balinese in repose. The face clearly shows the Siamese ancestry.*

Essentially, the Balinese is a long-haired Siamese with a softer voice. Efforts to produce such a cat were made by American breeders who crossed their Siamese with the Turkish Angora. When most of the resulting kittens were short-haired, the breeders were stymied—until it became known that many of these young kittens were carrying a recessive long-haired gene. Eventually, a pair of these cats were mated and the desired long-haired Siamese was produced. Except for its graceful movements, the Balinese has nothing to do with the island of Bali.

The Balinese is a colorpoint cat, with points ranging from seal to blue, lilac, and chocolate. (Red points, tortie points, and lynx points are called "Javanese"—see page 48—only by the Cat Fanciers' Association.) The

🐾 *Left: This detail of a delicately shaded apricot Balinese shows the breed's attractive wedge-shaped face and almond-shaped eyes.*

Appearance: This light-bodied cat resembles the svelte Siamese in every respect except that of its coat. Its head is a long, tapering wedge, set on a long, slender neck, and it has a straight nose whose color should harmonize with the coat color. Its almond-shaped eyes are a vivid sapphire blue and slant upward from the

ground color of the coat resembles ermine, rather than the fawnlike shades of the Siamese. The seal point Balinese has a cream-colored coat; the blue point, an ice-white coat with dark blue markings; the chocolate point, an ivory coat with chocolate markings; and the lilac point, an ice-white coat with rose-gray markings.

🐾 *As well as the distinctive head, eyes, and ears, the Balinese body shape also resembles that of the Siamese.*

Behavior: This is a good apartment cat, but it welcomes opportunities to enjoy the outdoors on a terrace or in a closed garden or cat run. It displays the acrobatic leaps of its Siamese forebears, but its voice is not loud or strident, probably due to the influence of its mixed ancestry, which includes the soft-voiced Turkish Angora. It prefers a temperate climate.

Temperament: Intelligent, active, and curious, this is an extroverted cat that enjoys company and may get into mischief if left alone too long. While the Balinese shows affection toward all family members, it tends to bond more closely with one person than with the others.

😺 Right and below: Sapphire-blue eyes are mandatory for all color forms of the Balinese.

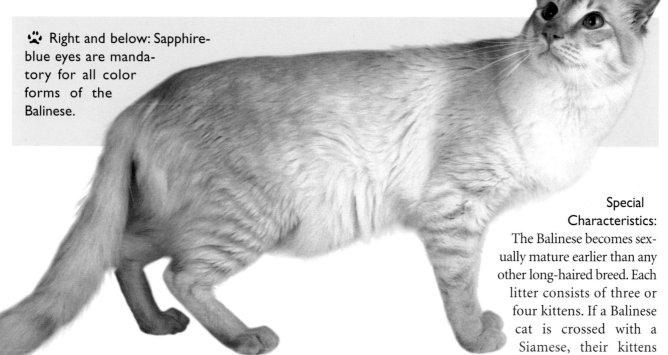

Special Characteristics: The Balinese becomes sexually mature earlier than any other long-haired breed. Each litter consists of three or four kittens. If a Balinese cat is crossed with a Siamese, their kittens show Siamese characteristics but have short, feltlike coats. The queen is an extremely good mother and plays with her young often. Since the Balinese has no downy undercoat, its fur does not mat; regular combing and brushing are all that is needed to maintain its appearance.

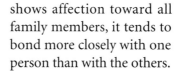

Paws for Thought

Wild on woodland ways your sires
Flashed like fires:
Fair as flame and fierce and fleet
As with wings on wingless feet
Shone and sprang your mother, free,
Bright and brave as wind or sea.

Free and proud and glad as they,
Here today
Rests or roams their radiant child,
Vanquished not, but reconciled.
Free from curb of aught above
Save the lovely curb of love.
　　　　　—Algernon Charles Swinburne

Origins: Attempts to breed a long-haired Siamese began in the United States during the 1930s and finally became successful some decades later. At first, the breed was called the Long-haired Siamese, but objections from breeders of the traditional Short-haired Siamese led to the adoption of the name Balinese. The new breed gained championship status in the United States in 1963. Faults for showing purposes include eye color other than blue, crossed eyes, an albino nose, weak hind legs, and the presence of an undercoat.

Javanese

There is much confusion over the cats known by the name Javanese, which refers to a separate group in North America, the UK, and other countries. In the United States, the Javanese is usually a form of Balinese, with different markings than the standard for the breed. Many U.S. registries make no distinction between the two. However, the Javanese is also known in the USA as the long-haired counterpart to the Colorpoint Shorthair, aside from its definition as a Balinese in other Siamese coat colors, including red point, tortie point, and lynx point. A number of U.S. catteries offer all three types of cats—Balinese, Siamese, and Javanese—for show and for sale.

Appearance: This graceful, long-limbed cat resembles the Balinese (or the Angora) in every respect except the colors and patterns.

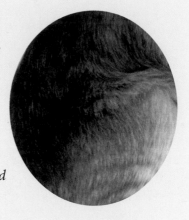

🐾 *The fur of the Javanese (Angora type) is fine and silky, of medium length. Like other semilonghairs, the hair is shorter on the head and sides of the body.*

The coat is long and silky, with no undercoat and no sign of the "collar" characteristic of long-haired breeds, requiring relatively little grooming.

Behavior: Sociable, extroverted, and inquisitive.

Temperament: Affable and adaptable.

Special Characteristics: According to the standard of the Governing Council of the Cat Fancy of Great Britain (GCCF), the breed called Javanese is an Abyssinian/Siamese hybrid that emerged from a breeding program aimed at re-creating the original Turkish Angora.

Origins: See Balinese, pages 47 and Angora, pages 42–43.

🐾 *This blue tabby Javanese/Angora shows the lines and facial characteristics of its Oriental ancestry.*

Munchkin

The irresistibly cute Munchkin is characterized by its short legs, which are the result of a spontaneous genetic mutation similar to that occurring in short-legged dogs like Corgis and Dachshunds.

Appearance: Munchkins can be short- or long-haired, with dense, plushlike fur, which can be of any color or pattern. They are medium-sized, thick-bodied cats, whose eyes are medium-large and rounded, and their tails are attractively plumed. The distinguishing feature of Munchkins is their disproportionately short legs.

🐾 *Because it is often seen sitting on its haunches, the Munchkin has acquired the nickname "kangaroo cat."*

Special Characteristics: Kittens with both short and long legs occur in the same litter.

Behavior: Active, energetic cats, their short stature does not stop Munchkins from leaping and climbing and does not appear to compromise their survival—though this is, understandably, the subject of some controversy. Munchkins are highly trainable and enjoy leash walking and retrieving games.

Temperament: Munchkins are gregarious, friendly cats that enjoy the company of their human family and mix well with dogs and other household pets. As if in response to their unusual size, Munchkins tend to remain kittenish in personality and are often very playful as mature cats.

Origins: Sightings of cats with dwarfed legs were reported in several parts of Europe before World War II, but Munchkins were first deliberately bred in Louisiana during the 1980s by Sandra Hochenedel, from a short-legged stray cat she named Blackberry. Munchkins have since gained recognition as a breed by TICA.

🐾 *The dwarfed legs of a Munchkin are a genetic trait.*

Maine Coon

The Maine Coon is believed to have originated from breeding between long-haired European cats and cats descended from those brought to North America by the original British settlers, making it the earliest American breed. This is a large, rugged cat that can tolerate cold climates because of its dense, shaggy coat and the slight undercoat that helps it to stay warm in harsh weather. It has been described as a "gentle giant" because its impressive size—it is one of the largest domestic cats—is accompanied by a calm disposition and an affectionate nature. The Maine Coon is one of the five most popular breeds in the United States, with 4,642 registered with CFA in 1999 and 1,851 with TICA.

Appearance: Male Maine Coons are much heavier than females, and both sexes develop slowly, not reaching full maturity until they are about four years old. The head is a broad, medium-length, modified wedge, with high cheekbones. Wide-set, expressive eyes are slightly slanted toward the outer base

Paws for Thought

"Roughly 5 percent of the sixteen billion pictures we take each year are of our animals. Even when a cat remains oblivious to the camera, the animal stands in for us, not simply to offer us a sense of scale, but to offer a sense of ourselves, cropped from the recklessly preoccupied world."

—Michael J. Rosen

of the ears, which are well tufted, as are the toe pads. Copper, green, or gold, the eyes do not necessarily conform to the coat color, which comes in all colors and patterns except colorpointed, solid chocolate, and solid lilac. (Tabby varieties often have white markings around the mouth and chin, while a white "locket," or neck marking, is characteristic of the breed.)

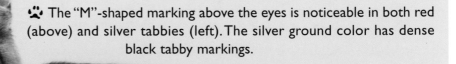

 The "M"-shaped marking above the eyes is noticeable in both red (above) and silver tabbies (left). The silver ground color has dense black tabby markings.

Left and overleaf, top: The brown tabby and white is descended from the more common brown tabby. Its coloration should be dominant, and the tabby markings clearly evident. Below, a handsome black and white.

Behavior: This healthy, good-natured cat is an excellent hunter and does not hesitate to go into the water. It is equally adaptable to life as a working farm cat or a valuable indoor companion, and it exhibits great presence in the show ring.

The Maine Coon has substantial, medium-length legs, and its body is so regularly proportioned that its silhouette has been described as capable of being inscribed in a rectangle. The paws are large and round, with pads that harmonize with the coat, and the long, plumy tail is thickly feathered to a blunt tip. The hair is short on the face and shoulders, but longer on the stomach and hind legs, where it forms britches. A frontal ruff is desirable in show-quality cats. Grooming should include combing and brushing about three times a week to remove dead hair and prevent matting.

Temperament: The Maine Coon is intelligent, discriminating, and loyal. Friendly and home-loving, it rarely strays, and tends to give itself most completely to one member of the family. It is very patient with children, and talkative, making soft chirping sounds that are very appealing.

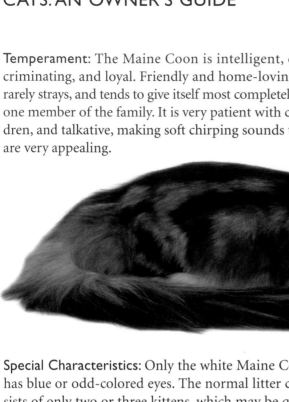

Special Characteristics: Only the white Maine Coon has blue or odd-colored eyes. The normal litter consists of only two or three kittens, which may be quite different from one another. In competition, faults include a scanty coat and flaccid musculature.

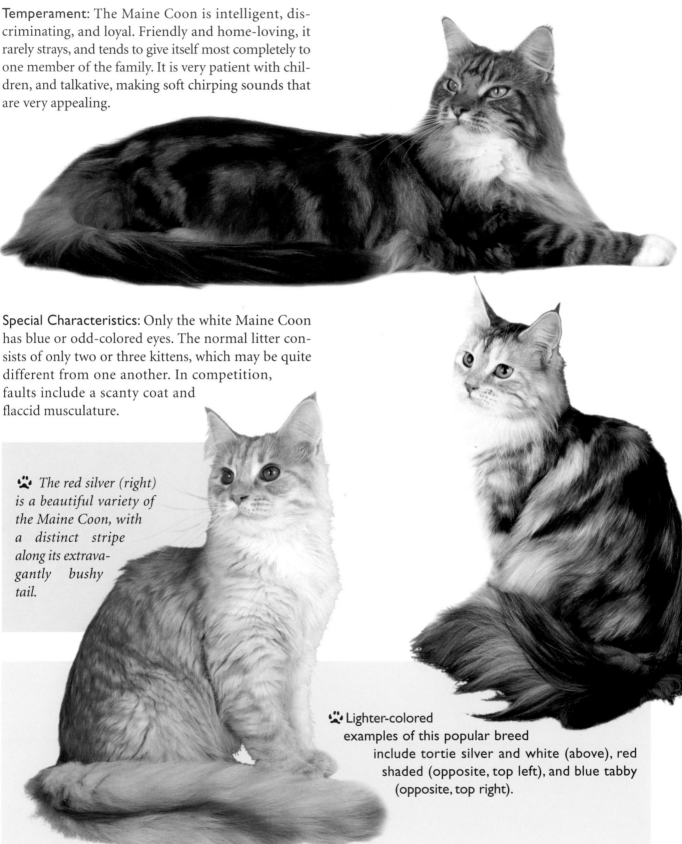

🐾 *The red silver (right) is a beautiful variety of the Maine Coon, with a distinct stripe along its extravagantly bushy tail.*

🐾 Lighter-colored examples of this popular breed include tortie silver and white (above), red shaded (opposite, top left), and blue tabby (opposite, top right).

Feline Facts

🐾 Their dense coats protect Maine Coons from the elements; in fact, some even like water and will happily play with a dripping tap.

Origins: Because of the similarity of the original Maine Coon cat to the raccoon, a popular fallacy held that the cat was actually descended from the raccoon—a cross that is genetically impossible.

🐾 *The blue smoke at left is a stunning example of the Maine Coon breed. Its color is comparatively rare.*

53

American Curl

Appearance: The breed's most distinctive feature is its backward-tipped ears, the result of a spontaneous mutation that proved to result from a dominant gene. The cat's body is medium-sized and elongated, and the head is a modified wedge with almond-shaped eyes. The elegant tail is wide at the base and beautifully plumed. Wide varieties in coat color include snow-white, silver tabby, red classic tabby, and colorpoint.

Feline Facts

🐾 All American Curl kittens are born with normal ears. It may take up to six months (or longer) to know which kittens will develop the characteristic curled ears.

Behavior: This good-natured cat will retain its playful disposition into adulthood and is known for its curiosity, adaptability, and positive interaction with both people and other animals.

The American Curl is a new and elegant breed that is seen in both short- and long-haired varieties. It takes its name from the distinctive backward curl of its ears, which apparently resulted from a spontaneous mutation (described under "Origins"). Various geneticists were consulted to verify that the trait was genetic and not acidental, and to set guidelines for early breeders. American Curls are considered "semi-foreign" in body type, as neither the distinctive triangular head and conformation of the Siamese, nor the other extreme of the Persian, are desired. The ideal look for show cats is close to the slender elegance of the Turkish Angora. Curls were first displayed in 1983 at a CFA show and are also shown in the International Cat Association.

🐾 *Above: A brown tabby American Curl; at right, a beautiful odd-eyed white. All coat colors and patterns are accepted for this breed. For show purposes, ear shape, degree of curl, positioning, and ear furnishings are assessed.*

Temperament: The American Curl has a sweet and friendly expression that conveys its loyal and affectionate nature. The breed's excellent temperament makes it suitable for households with children, and owners give these pets high marks for congenial companionship.

Special Characteristics: These graceful cats have oval eyes, slender limbs, and distinctive ears that stand upright for approximately one-third of their height and then curl back in a smooth arc to point to the back of the skull. Some breeders use a coin, set in the curve of the ear, to verify its correct curvature and size. Grooming is simple because the hair does not mat like that of most longhairs. The undercoat is minimal and there is no ruff. Regular combing and an occasional bath—best introduced early in the cat's life, so it becomes acclimated to the process—will keep its coat in good order.

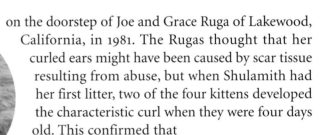

on the doorstep of Joe and Grace Ruga of Lakewood, California, in 1981. The Rugas thought that her curled ears might have been caused by scar tissue resulting from abuse, but when Shulamith had her first litter, two of the four kittens developed the characteristic curl when they were four days old. This confirmed that the trait was genetic.

Origins: The American Curl derives from a distinctive domestic cat named Shulamith, which was abandoned

 Above, a strikingly colored red American Curl; at right, an appealing brown spotted kitten showing the typical curled ear at an early stage.

Scottish Fold

The most immediately notice-able feature of this appeal-ing cat is its unusual ears, which fold for-ward to give it the appearance that it is wearing a cap. This is the result of a genetic mutation that was observed first, so far as we know, in the litter of a barn cat owned by the McRae family in the Tayside region of Scotland in 1961. A short-haired white kitten named Susie was the only one in the litter to display this mutation, and a local shep-herd named William Ross was intrigued by it. Two years later, Susie produced a litter containing two folded-ear kittens, one of which was given to the Ross family, who took an interest in developing a new breed with the help of a London breeder named Pat Turner. Over time, it became apparent that the ears of Scottish Fold kittens do not begin to fold until they are two to three weeks old.

Appearance: Now found in both short- and long-haired varieties, the Scottish Fold has often been bred with American or British Shorthairs. It has a wide, rounded head, a short neck, and a stocky, medium-sized body. Prominent cheeks are more noticeable in the male than in the female. Wide, well-rounded eyes divided by a broad nose, along with the folded ears, help to give this breed its appealing humanoid look. The coat is dense and springy and may be in twenty-three of the recognized colors of the American Shorthair. Eyes may be gold, green, hazel, or blue-green, depending upon the coat color, which the nose leather and paw pads should match.

Behavior: Outcrossings with the British and American Shorthair have contributed to the

This lovely pair of long-haired colorpoint Scottish Folds shows why the breed has become so popular.

placid disposition of the Scottish Fold. If allowed outdoors, it shows its prowess as a hunter by bringing back mice and other small animals.

Temperament: This is an affectionate and adaptable breed (now one of the ten most popular pedigreed cats in the United States) and usually adjusts to other pets with ease. It has a very small voice and is not very talkative.

Special Characteristics: Two Folds cannot be bred together, since the folded ears may be linked with a deformity that causes thickening of the hind legs and rigidity of the tail. Tapered and of medium length, the tail is manipulated gently in show cats to make sure it is flexible. The breed is still unrecognized by the Governing Council of the Cat Fancy of Britain because of concern about possible impaired hearing and/or ear mites and infections, although there is no evi-dence that Scottish Folds are any more prone to these problems than other cats.

Origins: Despite the controversy surrounding the Scottish Fold's origins, the breed was reg-istered by the CFA in 1974 and received cham-pionship status two years later. In fact, far more Scottish Folds are now bred in the United States than in Britain, although they were recognized by the Cat Association of Britain in 1983.

In kittens, like this blue cream (left), it takes about two to three weeks before the ears begin to fold over.

LaPerm

This new American breed resulted from a naturally occurring coat mutation found on a female farm cat in Oregon in the early 1980s. Appropriately named "Curly," her descendants come in both short- and long-haired varieties, with the latter being the most distinctive. Linda Koehl of Kloshe Cattery is the breed founder and the LaPerm Society of America offers information on the CFA's most recently recognized breed.

Appearance: The LaPerm is a medium-bodied cat of the type described as semiforeign (slightly elongated). The long coat forms curly ringlets all over the body and the cat comes in a wide variety of colors and patterns, including vibrant reds and bicolors. Curiously, sometime during kittenhood the LaPerm will usually lose all its hair; when the new coat grows in, it will be much curlier than before. This is a small breed, with males averaging seven to eight pounds and females five to six pounds. Even the whiskers and eyebrows are curly.

🐾 *This tortie, like all LaPerms, has an elongated body and large ears. Below, a lilac tortie and white.*

Behavior: The LaPerm is very doglike in its devotion, following its owner everywhere and coming at call. It is adaptable and travels well.

Feline Facts

🐾 An Oregon farm kitten born in 1982 was the founding mother of this curly-coated breed.

Temperament: This unusually affectionate breed is bright, playful, and quiet in its vocalizations.

Special Characteristics: Like the Poodle, the LaPerm's shedding is caught by its curls and rarely transferred to the environment. It requires little or no grooming.

Origins: Descended from hardy barn cats that have not been inbred, the LaPerm has no known genetic defects and is generally healthy and robust.

Short-Haired Breeds

Crossbreeding has resulted in a dazzling variety of coat lengths and types, from the nearly hairless Sphynx to the dense, flowing coat of the aristocratic Persian. Among the many attractions of the short-haired breeds is their relatively easy-care coats, which come in numerous colors and patterns, as seen on the following pages. In some cases, including the Devon Rex, whose fur is distinguished by loose, soft waves, the coat is the breed's major hallmark. Another feature of the short-haired breeds is the fact that their graceful body lines are more apparent than those of the long-haired cats.

This section focuses on some of the most popular and distinctive short-haired breeds, with keys to each one's appearance, behavior, temperament, special characteristics, and origins. Perhaps one of these appealing animals would be just right for you.

British Shorthair

🐾 *The striking patterns shown by these classic silver spotted and silver tabby cats were among the earliest developed for the British Shorthair and remain in high favor today.*

the British Shorthair's top popularity ranking. However, since World War II ended, it has steadily reassumed its place as a favorite in its native land and a highly prized breed in many other countries. It is believed that cats were introduced to Britain by the Romans. As evidence, clear imprints of cats' paws have been found in the tiles of Roman villas built in Britain during the first centuries of the Christian era.

According to *Simon & Schuster's Guide to Cats* (1983), Harrison Weir, a dedicated early cat breeder, "loved the prolific British street cat so much, he almost single-handedly created the British Shorthair." By the end of the nineteenth century, these animals had become extremely popular at the cat shows held at London's Crystal Palace. During the early decades of the twentieth century, though, the Persian Longhair usurped

🐾 *Above: A black British Shorthair; right, the cream variety is, in fact, a diluted red self color.*

Appearance: The British Shorthair is a medium- to large-sized, muscular cat with a compact body and a deep chest. Its head is broad, round, and massive, set on a short, thick neck. The forehead is slightly flat on top of the head and should not slope. This cat has a medium-sized nose that is broad and straight, with the nose leather compatible with the coat color. The well-developed muzzle has a definite stop behind the large, round whisker pads. The British Shorthair comes in no fewer than seventeen colors, excluding only solid chocolate, solid lilac, and colorpoint. The popu-lar tabby pattern includes all colors in the classic, mackerel, ticked, and spotted form. (Mackerel tabbies have narrow lines of a darker shade all over the body, with rings on the chest and tail, and even bars on the legs.) The short, dense coats of these animals have served them well in protecting them from cold, wet weather and the underbrush that once covered their original range.

🐾 *The tortoiseshell, like the chocolate tortie at left, is almost always female; below, silver tabby adult (left) and kitten.*

Feline Facts

🐾 It is believed that the Romans smuggled domestic cats out of Egypt, where they were worshipped as the goddess Bastet, and helped to spread them throughout the Roman Empire. The Egyptians were extremely possessive of their goddess, and in fact, built a shrine to her on an island, believing that her aversion to water would prevent her from straying.

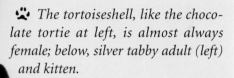

Temperament: The British Shorthair will play with children, dogs, and other cats when it becomes familiar with them. Resourceful and intelligent, it rarely encounters situations that it cannot handle with aplomb. Its calm, gentle nature makes it a loyal pet and an undemanding companion. The female is an especially excellent mother.

Above: a graceful tipped British Shorthair; at right (detail photo), a white cat with the typical round, full-cheeked face, has lovely green eyes with an alert expression.

Behavior: Adaptable to both indoor and outdoor living, the British Shorthair can tolerate cooler weather and needs little grooming beyond a weekly combing. Resistant to illness because of its hardy background, the cat has a strong sense of dignity and independence, while bonding closely with its family. Its genes have contributed good qualities to many other breeds, including the American Shorthair. It can be reserved, but it is not aloof.

Pointed cats like this red colorpoint should feature a blend of evenly mingled color on their points.

🐾 *The beautiful blue (right) is the most popular British Shorthair. Its eyes are large and rounded—usually copper- or gold-colored—and its dense, plushlike coat is a pleasure to touch. Indeed, this cat's fur appears almost velvety in texture.*

Special Characteristics: Although it often prefers a large environment with a yard or garden, this cat can adapt to almost any reasonable living conditions. For showing, several faults count heavily against the breed, including an irregular tail, nose stop, or long and fluffy coat. (During the early twentieth century, the British Shorthair was briefly crossed with the newly popular Persian, but the Persian traits were subsequently eliminated.)

🐾 *Cats with spotted markings, like this brown spotted British Shorthair, date back to ancient Egypt and are still favored for their "wild" look.*

Origins: Originally, this cat was known as the British Blue, which has been described as the aristocrat of British Shorthairs. The coat color is most attractive when it is a medium shade of blue and the coat is very short, with a plushlike appearance. The British cat fancy takes great pride in its Blue, and there is brisk competition with the Chartreux, or French Blue, which is similar in appearance and in its lengthy history. It was originally befriended by medieval monasteries as an excellent hunter and a congenial companion.

Exotic Shorthair

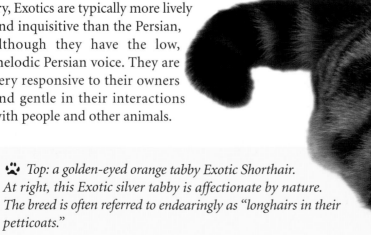

Recognized by most cat associations in the late 1960s, the Exotic Shorthair comes in all colors and has the appealing rounded face of the Persian, but with a short, plush coat. For some years prior to 1967, breeds other than the Persian were used by American Shorthair breeders to improve the coat, including Burmese and Abyssinians, but today the only outcross permitted is to the Persian.

Temperament: The Exotic is a loyal companion, quiet and playful, but also very good at entertaining itself. It does not demand constant attention and rarely vocalizes at all.

Special Characteristics: Exotic breeders and showers note that the cat's shorter coat makes it impossible to disguise any deviations

Feline Facts

🐾 A cat's body has more than 500 muscles, which accounts for its wonderful flexibility. The average cat can stretch to a third again of its length.

Appearance: The Exotic is a heavily boned and well-balanced cat with the typically cobby Persian body type set low on the legs, a broad, deep chest, and a level back. The double plush coat has an appealing teddy-bear look, and the round, massive head is set on a short, thick neck. The Exotic has full cheeks, broad jaws, and nose leather and paw pads in harmony with the coat color.

Behavior: As a result of their mixed ancestry, Exotics are typically more lively and inquisitive than the Persian, although they have the low, melodic Persian voice. They are very responsive to their owners and gentle in their interactions with people and other animals.

from the Persian standard with respect to nose, eye, ear, chin, and build. For example, there is no massive ruff to hide a neck that is too long and no flowing coat to conceal legs that are too long, or cowhocked.

Origins: The Exotic Shorthair may be called a manmade breed, since it resulted from the cross of Persians with American Shorthairs and other short-haired breeds.

 Top: a golden-eyed orange tabby Exotic Shorthair. At right, this Exotic silver tabby is affectionate by nature. The breed is often referred to endearingly as "longhairs in their petticoats."

European Shorthair

The common house and barn cat of Europeans for many generations, the European Shorthair is believed to have descended from the African Wild Cat brought north by the Romans some 2,000 years ago and/or from the native European Wild Cat. In different regions, it is known by many localized names, including Cyprus cat, Tiger cat (tabby is one of its commonest coat patterns), and Marbled cat.

or copper eyes; white, with yellow or copper eyes, and red or red-brown with orange eyes, as well as many variations on the classic tabby pattern.

Behavior: The European Shorthair is generally tolerant of new people, friendly toward people it knows, robust, and long-lived. It does not like to be confined, preferring to roam widely in large, open spaces.

🐾 *The eyes of European Shorthairs should be large, rounded, and well-spaced, with eye colors in keeping with the color of their coats. This blue self-colored example has beautiful copper eyes.*

Appearance: The European Shorthair's fur is short, thick, and finely textured. Its body is notably muscular and sturdy, with strong legs and medium-sized rounded paws. The head is round with a short nose, full cheeks, large eyes, and comparatively small pointed ears. The breed's colors and patterns range very widely, including black with yellow, orange,

Temperament: Due to their diverse ancestry, individual European Shorthairs vary widely in temperament, but this cat is almost always territorial and combative toward other cats in its chosen range. It is, however, affectionate and loyal toward caring owners.

Special Characteristics: Unless they have been spayed or neutered, the European Shorthair will reproduce more frequently than almost any other breed and tends also to produce much larger litters.

Origins: See the opening paragraph of this page.

🐾 *This breed is very similar to its British relatives, but it is less cobby in build.*

65

American Shorthair

This popular pedigreed cat was originally known in the United States as the Domestic Shorthair, a non-pedigree cat widely distributed as a household pet. The latter was brought to North America by European settlers, and its likeliest origin is in the handsome British Shorthair. Both are "working" cats, well-equipped to catch prey in their muscular jaws and endowed with strong limbs and an excellent sense of balance. Breeders have allowed their animals a wide range of natural selection to prevent inbreeding and to retain the American Shorthair's innate qualities of strength, stamina, and a wide variety of coat colors and markings.

Feline Facts

🐾 The American Shorthair is related to the European ships' cats that were used to kill rodents on voyages to North America. These cats have rounder faces and slightly larger bodies than their forebears.

🐾 *Brown tabbies like this delightful kitten and the handsome adult below are among the most common types of American Shorthair.*

Special Characteristics: The breed's coat colors and patterns are remarkably diverse, ranging from solid white, black, and blue, to shaded and silver, tabby, smoke and white, parti-color, and bicolor.

Origins: Shortly before persevering breeders changed this cat breed's name from Domestic Shorthair to American Shorthair in 1966, its star ascended when a silver tabby named Shawnee Trademark won "Best Cat of the Year" award in competition.

Appearance: The American Shorthair ranges in size from medium to large. Its compact, powerful body has a well-developed chest and strong hindquarters, with a broad head showing eyes and ears set well apart.

Behavior: This popular breed is highly valued for its adaptability to family life. It requires little specialized care and is readily trained to household routines, which provide it with a sense of security.

Temperament: Descriptions widely applied to the American Shorthair include healthy, friendly, robust, good-natured, and independent.

American Wirehair

Behavior: This breed has been described as even-tempered and circumspect. It readily attaches itself to its family, but enjoys tranquility and a sense of independence.

🐾 *All three of these American Wirehairs exhibit the dominant gene that makes their fur so different from a normal coat.*

The American Wirehair is a modern cat breed whose unmistakable, wiry coat was the result of a spontaneous mutation (described under "Origins"). Its fur is curly, or hooked, forming a medium-length coat that is coarser on the head, back, flanks, and tail; only the chin and underbelly are soft. According to the breed standard, most of the American Shorthair colors, except the patched tabby, are permissible. Faults in the breed include a long or soft coat, colors that could indicate hybridization, and a crooked tail.

Appearance: The American Wirehair's body is medium-sized, well-proportioned, and tends to be stocky and muscular. The head is round, with prominent cheeks, and the eyes are also round and of a color that harmonizes with the coat.

Temperament: American Wirehairs are curious and take a lively interest in their surroundings, indoors and out. Active and agile, sometimes bossy, they may have a tendency to dominate other cats.

Special Characteristics: Regular grooming enhances the Wirehair's coat, but brush and comb should be used in moderation, as the fur should have a curly rather than a wavy look.

Origins: The American Wirehair resulted from a spontaneous mutation in Verona, New York (1966), when two American Shorthair kittens were born with wiry, curly hair resembling that of a lamb's fleece. A series of crosses made by dedicated breeders resulted in the new breed, whose original sire was named, appropriately, Adam.

🐾 *Although it may feel odd to stroke their wiry coats, these cats enjoy the attention.*

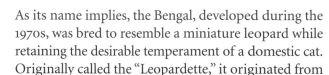

Bengal

As its name implies, the Bengal, developed during the 1970s, was bred to resemble a miniature leopard while retaining the desirable temperament of a domestic cat. Originally called the "Leopardette," it originated from

Behavior: Independent by nature, the Bengal is a born hunter and seems to enjoy wading in the water, even to jumping in the bathtub with its owner! It is also a vigorous climber and needs a good deal of space.

Temperament: Bengals have been described as intelligent, alert, affectionate, determined, and outgoing. Their vocalizations differ from those of most domestic cats in having several elements that are more commonly heard in wildcats.

Special Characteristics: According to TICA standards, Bengals are not authorized to mate with any other breeds. If they are being shown, any sign of challenge will disqualify them. Their fur is thick and luxurious, with clearly marked random spots; blotchy horizontal shoulder streaks are also desirable.

Origins: Eight female cats crossbred from an Asian Leopard Cat and domestic shorthairs were bred by Jean Mills to a feral orange cat with deep brown spots and a brown-spotted tabby shorthair. The resulting offspring had developed into the Bengal breed within ten years and were first exhibited at TICA cat shows in 1984-85.

crosses between a wild Asian cat (*Felis bengalensis)* and domestic shorthairs. Mrs. Jean Mills was the first breeder, followed by Dr. Gregg Kent, who produced crosses between a male Leopard Cat and a female Egyptian Mau. Other domestic breeds that have been used to produce the Bengal include the Ocicat, Abyssinian, Bombay, and British Shorthair.

Appearance: The Bengal is a large cat (males can weigh up to twenty-two pounds) with a wonderful spotted or marbled coat, a muscular body, high hindquarters, and oval eyes.

🐾 *A Bengal's fur pattern (above; detail right) can resemble that of a leopard, with large spots that form rings or rosettes and are distributed randomly on the body.*

Chartreux

History tells that the beautiful blue Chartreux lived with, and were named for, the Carthusian monks of France. More recent evidence indicates that they were given the same name as a well-known Spanish wool because of the dense, wooly texture of their coats. However, they have always been associated with France, where their presence was recorded as early as the sixteenth century.

Appearance: The Chartreux is famous for its "smile," because the rounded head tapers to a narrowed muzzle, which gives the cat the appearance of smiling. It has a robust body, with broad shoulders and a deep chest, and finely boned, medium-short legs. Its blue fur is unique in being thick and springy like a sheep's, due to a dense undercoat, and the desired coat breaks at the neck, chest, and flanks. Eye color ranges from gold to copper, and the ears are of medium size, set high and erect on the head.

The blue-gray coloring of this cat is distinctive, and no other colors are recognized.

Special Characteristics: The Chartreux does not usually reach physical maturity until about three years of age. The double coat should not be brushed: Breeders recommend running one's fingers through the fur every day, which also contributes, like other forms of grooming and petting, to the bond between cat and owner.

Origins: As a monastery cat for members of the Carthusian order, the Chartreux was highly prized for protecting valuable manuscripts from damage by rats.

Feline Facts

An unusual naming system has been developed for this breed, whereby each year is represented alphabetically by a letter (omitting K, Q, W, X, Y, Z). The cat's name, therefore (e.g., Norman), reveals the year in which it was born, in this case, 1977.

Behavior: The Chartreux is almost doglike in its devotion to its owner, following him or her from room to room and often learning to fetch toys. It will usually respond to its name and is very intelligent and alert.

Temperament: This is a quiet breed, which makes chirping noises rather than meowing at things it finds interesting. Many Chartreux appear to be attracted by television, and reportedly, some enjoy participating in telephone conversations by chewing on the cord—certainly not to be encouraged!

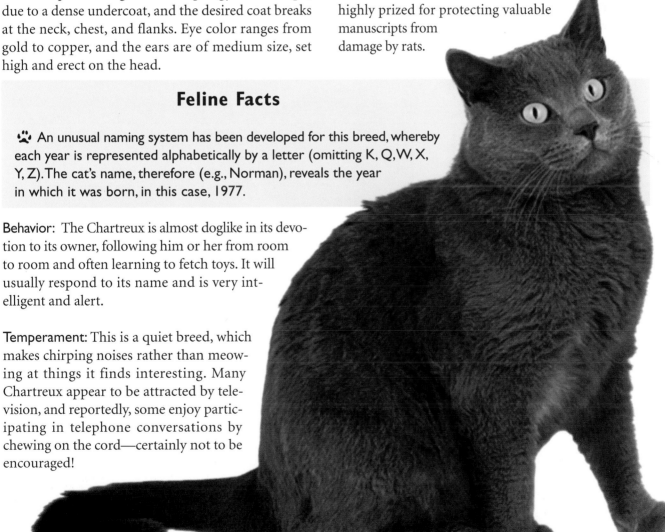

Bombay

This handsome breed, developed in the late 1950s and early 1960s, is still rare outside the United States. It was named for India's black leopard because of its sleek, satiny coat. In fact, the jet-black coat and its quality are considered so important that 50 percent of the points awarded to a show-quality Bombay are based on these factors. Bombay kittens may be born with rusty-brown coats, but they will mature to the requisite black. Most fanciers prefer brilliant, copper-colored eyes to the golden eyes that also occur in this breed.

🐾 *The Bombay is a majestic animal with a solid jet-black coat that is short, sleek, and very shiny.*

Appearance: The Bombay is a medium-sized cat with a round head and eyes and a short muzzle. The ears are gently rounded at the tips and perk up immediately when the cat hears a sound, showing its alertness. Like most cats, however, it deplores loud noises in the environment. Both its nose and its paw pads are black. The Bombay exemplifies the self- or solid-colored cat, which means that the hair is one color from root to tip. Males of this breed are noticeably larger than females.

Behavior: This is a born house cat that will live indoors happily all its life. Bright and agile, the Bombay thrives on company, but it may pine and misbehave when left alone too long. It sheds very little and needs only a brief daily combing to remove shedded hair.

Temperament: Owners vow that this cat almost never stops purring. It is active, friendly, and responsive—ideal for a stay-at-home owner—and enjoys games and fetching. Its soft voice is very appealing. The Bombay thrives best in a warm climate.

Special Characteristics: The Bombay has an elegant tail of medium length and a tall, graceful body. Its appetite is moderate, because it burns relatively few calories, but the kittens—four or five to a litter—are voracious eaters.

Origins: The breed resulted from successful crossings between the Burmese and the American Shorthair. Kentucky breeder Nikki S. Horner was instrumental in having the Bombay recognized, and it was awarded championship status by the CFA in 1976. At this writing, the breed is still awaiting recognition in other countries, including Britain.

Feline Facts

🐾 Most cats have from twenty-five to thirty long whiskers that grow in four rows from the side of the mouth to above the eyes. Attached to nerves in the skin, they act as sense organs. This gave rise to the erroneous belief that cats use their whiskers to measure a space through which they can pass.

Singapura

The delicately colored Singapura, small and beautifully proportioned, is another relatively new breed on the U.S. show scene that is gaining rapidly in popularity. It thrives best in a warm climate and will live happily indoors. Its plushlike coat needs only occasional combing. The breed was accorded championship status in 1988, and astonishingly, it went on to win twenty-two grand championship titles in its second season of showing.

🐾 *The Singapura's ground color is ivory with brown ticking, also called sepia agouti.*

Temperament: Sweet-tempered and playful, the Singapura retains these qualities into adulthood, becoming a highly valued member of the family. It is also an effective hunter and is best kept indoors in the interest of birds and other small wildlife.

Special Characteristics: The Singapura's sleek, close-lying coat feels like satin. According to *Cats: The Little Guides*, "The ground color is old ivory, with each hair on the back, top of the head, and flanks ticked with at least two bands of a deep brown separated by bands of warm old ivory (this is also known as agouti ticking)."

Appearance: This cat's sepia coloring distinguishes it from any other breed. The coat is a ticked warm beige and the large, almond-shaped eyes, outlined with dark brown, are very expressive. The Singapura is small and symmetrical, with muscular legs tapering to small, oval feet and a slender tail darker than the rest of the coat.

Origins: Little is known of the breed's origin, except that the foundation stock of all U.S. Singapuras comprises four cats owned by a single American breeder. Reportedly, they have some connection with the street cats of Singapore, but this is not certain.

Feline Facts

🐾 *Singapura,* the Malaysian name for Singapore, may be this cat's place of origin. It is believed to descend from feral cats that live in Southeast Asia.

Behavior: The Singapura is moderately active, curious, and affectionate. It bonds quickly with its owners and gets along well with other animals. The females are known as especially attentive and loving mothers.

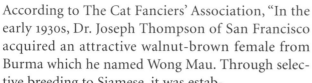

Burmese

According to The Cat Fanciers' Association, "In the early 1930s, Dr. Joseph Thompson of San Francisco acquired an attractive walnut-brown female from Burma which he named Wong Mau. Through selective breeding to Siamese, it was established that the Burmese is a distinct breed."

Appearance: The Burmese has a very short coat with a satin-like texture that requires little grooming. The U.S. Burmese is somewhat rounder and stockier in build than its British counterpart, which was introduced from the United States in 1947. (In the U.K., the Burmese has developed along the lines of its streamlined ancestor, the Siamese, in a spectrum of new colors.) U.S. standards call for a compact, medium-sized, well-boned body type, with a rounded chest and a back that is level from shoulders to hips. The head is medium-sized, in a rounded wedge shape with a short, well-developed muzzle. The breed is especially well known for its large, well-rounded, expressive eyes, which are set far apart and a deep gold in color.

🐾 Note the color contrast between the lighter lilac tortie Burmese and the original brown.

Later, lighter-colored kittens among Burmese litters led to a request from breeders for recognition of "dilute" colors, which the CFA has recognized as sable, champagne, blue, and platinum—the only colors for showing in America.

🐾 *This fur detail from a blue Burmese is typically short and glossy. The fur has a satiny feel that is a delight to stroke.*

Special Characteristics: Burmese are good with children and tolerant of dogs; if introduced to traveling by car at an early age, most learn to enjoy it.

Behavior: Like the Chartreux, the Burmese is noted for its attachment to its owner/s, shadowing their steps and learning to fetch toys and perform other "doglike" tricks.

Origins: There is no doubt that at least one founding member of this breed originated in Burma, where cats have been recorded for at least 500 years. However, the modern breed was originally developed in the U.S. before World War II.

Those who know the breed well advise that it should never be let outdoors, because of its trusting nature, which puts it at risk of theft and attack by other animals.

🐾 *Above: an elegant cream Burmese. Lilacs (left) are pale as kittens and develop a lovely gray color as they grow. Their pads change from a pale pink to lavender pink.*

Temperament: Burmese kittens are very lively and remain playful well into adulthood. Their high level of intelligence becomes more apparent as they grow, and they vocalize with their humans in soft, sweet voices, aided and abetted by their appealing eyes.

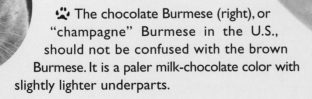

🐾 The chocolate Burmese (right), or "champagne" Burmese in the U.S., should not be confused with the brown Burmese. It is a paler milk-chocolate color with slightly lighter underparts.

Asian

 The Asian black smoke, shown at right, is a recent British breed created by mating Burmilla (see opposite page) with Burmese.

The Asian group of cat breeds describes a number of variants of Burmese cats bred primarily in Britain that display certain colors, patterns, and coat lengths, including numerous tabbies and smokes that are short-haired or semilong-haired. The GCCF includes the Burmilla, Bombay, and Tiffanie (not to be confused with the Tiffany/Chantilly) in the Asian group, but these are not universally recognized as separate breeds.

The *Bombay* (see page 70) has been recognized in the USA since 1976, but the U.S. Bombay has developed with slightly different characteristics from the British version, illustrated below, because the American Bombay breed originated with a cross between Burmese and American Shorthairs.

The *Asian Burmilla* is a relatively recent British breed resulting from an unplanned mating between a male Silver Chinchilla and a female Lilac Burmese.

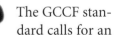

The GCCF standard calls for an agouti coat, which appears in both standard and silver versions, either tipped or shaded in one of thirteen colors. The body is Burmese in conformation. The eyes are green and are characterized by dark "eyeliner" markings, while the nose leather is brick red. Burmillas may be short-haired or semilong-haired.

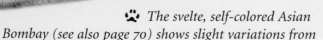 *The svelte, self-colored Asian Bombay (see also page 70) shows slight variations from the U.S. breed. It has been bred in the UK using British-type Burmese and black British Shorthairs. However, its sleek patent-leather coat conforms to CFA standards for the Bombay.*

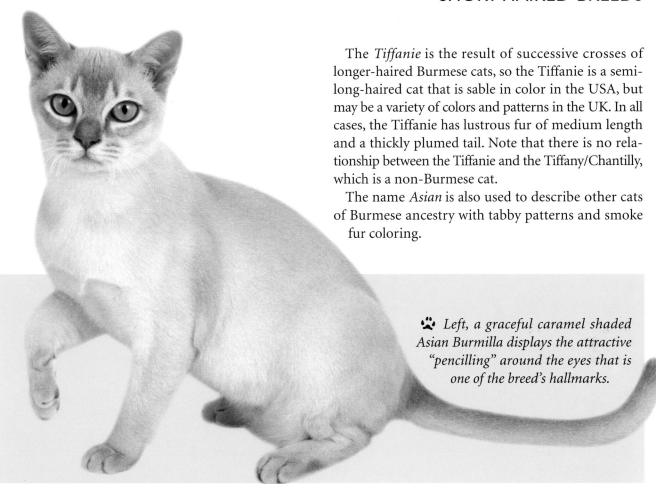

The *Tiffanie* is the result of successive crosses of longer-haired Burmese cats, so the Tiffanie is a semi-long-haired cat that is sable in color in the USA, but may be a variety of colors and patterns in the UK. In all cases, the Tiffanie has lustrous fur of medium length and a thickly plumed tail. Note that there is no relationship between the Tiffanie and the Tiffany/Chantilly, which is a non-Burmese cat.

The name *Asian* is also used to describe other cats of Burmese ancestry with tabby patterns and smoke fur coloring.

🐾 *Left, a graceful caramel shaded Asian Burmilla displays the attractive "pencilling" around the eyes that is one of the breed's hallmarks.*

The Asian ticked tabby also has the coat pattern described as agouti, that is, each hair is banded with black, brown, or yellow.

🐾 *Above, this Asian ticked cat shows its family resemblance to the Asian Burmilla, top. At left, a chocolate shaded Tiffanie.*

Ocicat

This relatively recent American breed resembles an ocelot in having the spotted markings of the handsome wild cat, but with the disposition of the domestic cat. The first kitten appeared in a litter bred by Michigan breeder Virginia Daly, who had crossed a ruddy Abyssinian with a seal-point Siamese. Born in 1964, the kitten was named Tonga and nicknamed "Ocicat" by the breeder's daughter for its resemblance to the spotted wild cat.

Appearance: The Ocicat is a medium- to large-sized animal with a long, well-muscled body that appears lithe and athletic. The head is a modified wedge, and the broad muzzle ends in a strong chin. The neck arches gracefully, and the large, almond-shaped eyes are wide set. The coat is short, smooth, and finely textured, with all the hairs ticked in a banded pattern except the tip of the long, slim tail, which is tipped with a solid color. The coat's ground color ranges from white to ivory to orange, and the thumbprint-size spots are accepted in more than a dozen colors. A tabby-type "M" extends from the forehead over the head.

Behavior: Ocicats are sociable animals, displaying many traits common to their Abyssinian, Siamese, and American Shorthair ancestors. They enjoy being around people and other animals, especially those with a similarly high energy level.

Temperament: While they are capable of forming strong attachments to their families, Ocicats are not demanding. They are also bright and easily trained. In general, they are outgoing and rarely shy with visitors to the household.

Special Characteristics: Despite its "wild" appearance, the Ocicat is very affectionate and dislikes being left alone for long periods of time. It does best living indoors in a warm climate.

Origins: The Ocicat resulted from the spontaneous mutation described in the opening paragraph, above.

🐾 Color variations include the lilac ocicat (above) and the darker chocolate at right, with its distinct pattern of spots. Eye color varies, but blue eyes are not permitted.

Egyptian Mau

This cat, with its slender, graceful body and distinct pattern of random spots on a lighter background, has been clearly identified as one of those pictured in ancient Egyptian wall paintings and sculptures. It is thought that the word "Mau" derives from the characteristic call "meow," which knows no language barrier.

Temperament: This cat will become very attached to its owner, and is loyal, active, and playful. It is believed to have a good memory and does not readily transfer its affection to a new owner.

🐾 Both of the silver Egyptian Maus pictured here (fur detail, left) show the distinct pattern common to the breed, which is the only natural strain of spotted cat. The two lines at each side of the face are also characteristic of the breed.

Appearance: The Egyptian Mau is the only natural strain of spotted cat, and its appearance is striking. It is a medium-sized, very strong animal with a slightly rounded wedge-shaped head; pointed ears set well apart; and vivid green, almond-shaped eyes (the eye color develops as the Mau matures). Its legs are slender, with small, oval feet, and the handsome coat is medium length and glossy. U.S. standards mandate three colors for showing: silver, bronze, and smoke. The black Mau can be used in a breeding program, but is not eligible for championship showing.

Behavior: The Egyptian Mau is a very intelligent creature, as seen in its characteristic wide-eyed, alert, expression, and it is unique among cats in that its tail "wags" rapidly when it is happy.

Special Characteristics: The Egyptian Mau vocalizes in a soft, melodious voice, especially when it is content. It has the regal bearing of its distant ancestors: one can readily imagine it seated gracefully on a pedestal.

Origins: Believed to have originated in Cairo, the American breed is based upon three animals imported from Egyptian stock in 1956. Later, the gene pool was broadened, and the breed gained championship status in the U.S. in 1977.

🐾 *The Mau has beautiful markings.*

Abyssinian

This active, alert, and energetic cat is one of the five most popular breeds in the United States. The silky coat requires little maintenance and colors range from ruddy to red, blue, and fawn. The Abyssinian appears to shimmer, especially in sunlight, because the solid color that one sees is an optical illusion. Each hair has bands of black ticking that alternate with bands in shades of brown, orange, or tan (silver is accepted in Europe).

Appearance: This medium-sized cat is lithe and muscular. Males weigh eight to ten pounds; females, five to seven. The relatively large ears, set well apart, and almond-shaped eyes resemble those of cats seen in ancient Egyptian art.

🐾 In recent years, there has been substantial development of the Abyssinian breed (eye detail, left). The lilac variety (right) is now relatively common.

Behavior: Abyssinians are extremely energetic and make wonderful companions to those who can keep up with them. They demand good company and are extremely loyal and entertaining.

🐾 *The fawn kitten at left and usual kitten at far left have darker masks and ticking than adults. The ticking does not appear until they are more than three weeks old.*

Temperament: Most Abys are easily leash-trained (the better to see what's going on out there), and they enjoy participating in family activities of all kinds. As a whole, they are not lap cats.

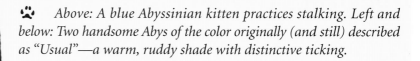 *Above: A blue Abyssinian kitten practices stalking. Left and below: Two handsome Abys of the color originally (and still) described as "Usual"—a warm, ruddy shade with distinctive ticking.*

Origins: It is believed that the Abyssinian arose in Southeast Asia, possibly as far east as Indochina. The original pair was brought from Abyssinia to England about 1860, and the merits of the tomcat, Zula, were transmitted to numerous offspring.

Special Characteristics: The Abyssinian is better suited to a house rather than a small apartment—preferably one with sheltered access to the outdoors. He is an excellent tree climber and likes to scale the heights and bask in the expected applause. He has a hearty appetite and may beg for table scraps in addition to his regular diet. Don't be persuaded to overfeed.

Siamese/Colorpoint Shorthair

The elegant Siamese is one of the five most popular breeds in the United States. It is distinguished by its svelte, long-legged body, large ears, brilliant blue, almond-shaped eyes, loud voice, and the darker colors (known as points) on the face, ears, tail, and legs.

The ground color, pure white at birth, ranges in maturity from fawn to cream. The original colorpoint was the seal point, made famous—or notorious—in Walt Disney's *Lady and the Tramp*, in which a pair of mischievous Siamese climbed curtains, destroyed the furniture, and stalked the baby. They sang a duet that began, "We are Siamese, if you please; we are Siamese, if you don't please." Here, they played the villains of the piece and parodied several qualities that have made the Siamese known for its good-humored—sometimes boisterous—antics, high intelligence, and insistent demands for attention.

Siamese cats apparently arrived in Europe in the late nineteenth century when a pair was presented to visiting dignitaries by the royal family of Siam (now Thailand). They had been bred for centuries by Buddhist monks in their temples as animals belonging exclusively to royalty, so the gift was considered a great honor.

🐾 *The seal point (left) is the classic color associated with the Siamese, and at one time it was the only color recognized.*

Appearance: The ideal Siamese is slender and refined, with a medium-sized, tubular body tapering down to a long, straight tail. Its physique combines fine bones and firm muscles, which give it great agility, especially for amazing leaps to high places. Its hips are the same width as its shoulders, and its legs are notably long and graceful. The head is a long, tapering wedge with a fine muzzle and the large ears are set well apart. Medium-sized, almond-shaped eyes slant upward from the nose.

🐾 *This cream tabby point is keeping an eye on the events going on around. Curious, like all Siamese cats, he is an intelligent animal and loves being part of the family.*

The best-known colorpoints besides seal are blue, chocolate, and lilac (also called "frost point"). When several other colors were introduced more recently, debate raged in the cat fancy as to whether the red, tortie, and lynx points should be recognized. Eventually, some associations accepted the latter colors as Siamese, while others, including the CFA, called them Colorpoint Shorthairs.

Behavior: Centuries of close relationships with people have made the Siamese an unusually gregarious cat; they are at home almost everywhere. Despite their exotic looks, they can be rambunctious and even destructive if left alone too long.

🐾 *Right: It is easy to see the development of the points on this chocolate kitten. They are not fully colored until the age of one year. If the points develop too early, they will be too dark at maturity.*

Temperament: Always curious, the Siamese has an agenda that keeps it looking around the next corner. Many cat fanciers consider it the most intelligent breed. The Siamese soon learns its name and demands inclusion in family activities. It can be trained to walk on a leash and even to play fetch and is generally good with children.

Special Characteristics: The Siamese is generally considered the king of cat communicators. It is extremely vocal, and females in heat can be heard a block away. Unless you are planning to breed your own male or female Siamese, it is a good idea to have the animal sterilized, which lowers the noise level considerably

without impairing the cat's delightful personality. This is a long-lived breed, which may live from fifteen to twenty years barring accident or illness.

Origins: We know that the Siamese is of Asiatic origin, but we are not sure of the wild species from which it has descended. Old prints show the earliest Siamese known to us with a striped coat characteristic of jungle cats. However, the domestic cats still found in Thailand bear little resemblance to the animals that have evolved over the past century for breeding and showing in the West. They are stockier, with round heads, crossed eyes, and crooked tails, any of which traits would disqualify them from today's competitions.

🐾 *Left: This cream tabby exudes the slender grace that characterizes her breed. Note the intelligent expression of the vivid blue eyes. The cream Siamese has coloring so subtle that it is sometimes difficult to recognize as a true colorpoint.*

The Orientals

Beginning in the 1950s, British breeders took the lead in creating several short- and long-haired breeds collectively known as Orientals from their sleek lines,

🐾 *The Havana (left) was known in Britain as the Chestnut Brown Foreign until 1970. It originated in the early 1950s with the cross-breeding described below.*

Appearance: The Havana, or Havana Brown, was the first all-brown cat, resulting from crosses in Britain during the early 1950s between a seal-point Siamese and a short-haired black cat with Siamese forebears. Originally known as Chestnut Brown Foreigns, these cats were the foundation stock of the Havana Brown, imported to the U.S. during the mid-1950s, where the breed diverged along sturdier lines than its British prototypes. The distinctive color has been compared to that of a fine Havana cigar—a rich, even shade of warm mahogany.

🐾 The cinnamon (below) is a self- or solid-colored cat with no white fur (detail right).

based on Siamese parentage. Among these breeds were the *Havana* (or *Havana Brown*), the *Foreign White*, and the *Oriental Black*.

Like its close cousins, the Oriental Black is an elegant, ebony-colored cat featuring the sleek, slender lines seen in the Siamese and a very muscled body. The head is a refined wedge shape, and the ears are large and pointed, open at the base. Almond-shaped eyes slant upward from the nose and are usually green, as with the Havana, but white Orientals may have blue, green, or odd eyes. The coats of the Oriental Shorthairs are short, fine, and lie close to the body.

🐾 *At right, a red silver shaded Oriental shows the angular, svelte conformation of its type.*

The Foreign White type was developed by another British cat breeder and geneticist whose work

🐾 Feline Facts

The British-bred Foreign White was imported to the United States in 1962; there it was accepted as the Oriental Shorthair, along with other similar "foreign-type" cats.

was aimed at producing a blue-eyed white cat of the same foreign type, but without the deafness associated with some other blue-eyed cats. Beginning in 1962, he succeeded in breeding such cats, and two well-known Siamese breeders from the U.S. were so enamored of the Foreign White that they sought acceptance in their country for this and similar "foreign-type" cats under the collective name of Oriental Shorthair in 1972. The breed was accepted for championship showing in the U.S. in 1977.

🐾 *Other colors of Oriental Shorthairs include chocolate, blue, and lilac (originally known as Oriental Lavender).*

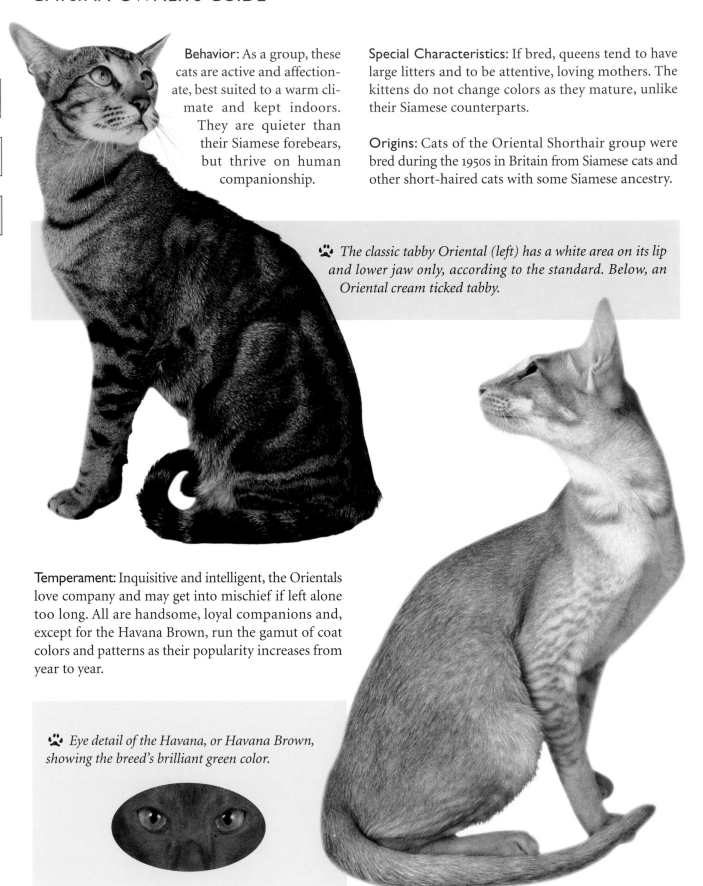

Behavior: As a group, these cats are active and affectionate, best suited to a warm climate and kept indoors. They are quieter than their Siamese forebears, but thrive on human companionship.

Special Characteristics: If bred, queens tend to have large litters and to be attentive, loving mothers. The kittens do not change colors as they mature, unlike their Siamese counterparts.

Origins: Cats of the Oriental Shorthair group were bred during the 1950s in Britain from Siamese cats and other short-haired cats with some Siamese ancestry.

The classic tabby Oriental (left) has a white area on its lip and lower jaw only, according to the standard. Below, an Oriental cream ticked tabby.

Temperament: Inquisitive and intelligent, the Orientals love company and may get into mischief if left alone too long. All are handsome, loyal companions and, except for the Havana Brown, run the gamut of coat colors and patterns as their popularity increases from year to year.

Eye detail of the Havana, or Havana Brown, showing the breed's brilliant green color.

Snowshoe

This handsome cat, still comparatively rare, is a hybrid of the Birman, the Siamese, and the bicolor American Shorthair.

Behavior: This well-behaved cat is ideally suited to indoor living and prefers a warm climate. It is active and playful by nature and a good all-around companion. It has a soft, melodic voice that is very pleasing.

Temperament: The Snowshoe is adaptable to many circumstances and shows the best qualities of its forebears, being outgoing, sturdy, and affectionate. It gets along well with other animals and enjoys life to the fullest.

🐾 *An appealing blue point Snowshoe kitten (above), and two adults with the breed's distinctive markings.*

As the name suggests, it is distinguished by its four white feet; it also has a white throat and white facial markings. Only two colors are allowed: blue point and seal point. Breeders strive for kittens displaying the preferred amount of white in the desirable patterns.

Appearance: As one would imagine, this cat combines the substantial body of the American Shorthair with the body length of the Siamese. It is muscular, powerful, and athletic in appearance, with a neck of medium length and a slightly rounded, wedge-shaped face with high-set cheekbones. Eyes are large, round, and a vivid blue. Only an occasional combing is required to keep the Snowshoe looking its best.

Special Characteristics: The preferred foot markings are white "boots" that extend only to the bend of the ankle on the forepaws and to just below the hocks on the back feet.

Origins: Both seal points and blue points with symmetrical white markings have often occurred spontaneously, and a group of dedicated breeders decided, in the late 1960s, to work toward this ideal and to set a standard for the new breed they called the Snowshoe. The breed was registered by both the Cat Fanciers' Federation and the American Cat Association by 1974. It gained championship status in 1982, but at this writing not all associations have accepted it for championship status.

Russian Blue

Believed to have originated in the far north of Russia and the Scandinavian Peninsula, the Russian Blue probably reached Europe during the late Middle Ages aboard merchant ships from these northern climes.

> "Cats are absolute individuals, with their own ideas about everything, including the people they own."

Appearance: The Russian Blue is an elegant cat, lithe and graceful, but well-muscled and firm. The head is a modified wedge with a blunt muzzle, and the nose leather is slate-gray in the U.S. and blue in Britain. The wide-set eyes are attractive and rounded, emerald-green in color. The cat has long, fine-boned legs with small, slightly rounded paws, and the tail is long and tapering. Perhaps its most distinctive feature is its beautiful dense, double coat, the guard hairs of which are tipped with silver, giving the Russian Blue a luminous silvery aura.

The beautiful blue fur of this cat has a seal-like quality and a distinctive silvery gloss.

Behavior: This is a gentle, affectionate breed, which develops strong ties to its owner or family. A good companion, it is playful and intelligent, learning how to open doors and to fetch.

Temperament: Although somewhat shy, the Russian Blue soon learns to get along well with children and other pets. It vocalizes in a quiet voice and is healthy and easy to care for.

Special Characteristics: The coat is so dense that it will hold a pattern traced in it until smoothed away. Regular hand grooming, or an occasional combing, will keep the Russian Blue looking its best. A damp chamois glove brings up the coat's luster.

Origins: It is known that a Russian Blue competed in Britain in 1875 in a class for all-blue cats of various types, but the breed was not recognized as such until 1912.

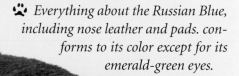

Everything about the Russian Blue, including nose leather and pads. conforms to its color except for its emerald-green eyes.

Korat

Not dissimilar in appearance to the Russian Blue, the Korat is a native of Thailand and named for one of its provinces. The name Korat means "good luck," and the cats were occasionally bestowed as gifts to visiting dignitaries, but never sold. It is also known as the Si-Siwat.

Appearance: The Korat is a solidly built, muscular cat with a short, dark-blue coat tipped with silver. Males are heavier than females, and both are semicobby in body type, with broad chests and curved backs. The head is distinctively heart-shaped and very broad across the eyes. The adult Korat's eyes are large, prominent, and green, with unusual depth and expression, although they may be yellow or amber before the cat reaches maturity. The forelegs are shorter than the back, and the paws are oval-shaped, with pinkish-lavender pads. The coat is short, single, and glossy, lying close to the body.

🐾 *This delicately shaded cat, and the one at the bottom of the page, are known in Britain as Thai lilacs. At left, a dark blue silver-tipped Korat.*

Special Characteristics: The Korat is a relative of the Burmese and prospers in a warm climate. It enjoys access to the outdoors, preferably in a sheltered environment.

Origins: Paintings of this unique breed have been found in Thailand's national library in manuscripts dating back to the mid-fourteenth century.

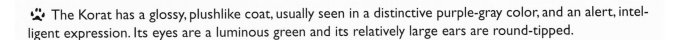

🐾 The Korat has a glossy, plushlike coat, usually seen in a distinctive purple-gray color, and an alert, intelligent expression. Its eyes are a luminous green and its relatively large ears are round-tipped.

Behavior: The Korat is a gentle animal that enjoys being stroked and groomed with a daily combing to remove dead hair. Apparently, its senses of sight, smell, and hearing are even more acute than those of the average cat.

Temperament: These cats are easily startled by sudden noises, but they enjoy playing with their humans and are surprisingly good with children.

Tonkinese

The beautiful, softly colored Tonkinese originated in Canada during the early 1960s as the result of crossing a seal point Siamese and a sable Burmese. The new breed shares some of the best features of the parent breeds and could be described as a fuller-bodied Siamese with aquamarine rather than blue eyes and a definite contrast between body color and points.

Appearance: The body color of the Tonkinese is darker than that of the Siamese, and the lustrous coat is medium-short, lying close to the body. The ideal body shape is intermediate between the Siamese and the Burmese—neither extremely svelte nor stocky. The almond-shaped eyes slant up along the high cheekbones, which are gently planed, and the muzzle is blunt. For U.S. show purposes, only five colors are allowed: champagne mink, blue mink, honey mink, natural mink, and platinum mink. British standards allow much wider color variations.

Behavior: The Tonkinese is an indoor cat that needs a warm climate. It is very talkative and responsive, keeping owners entertained with its active, inquisitive ways.

Left: A blue tabby Tonkinese shows the attractive features of both its Siamese and Burmese forebears.

This elegant brown tabby captures the spirit of the Tonkinese—intelligent, lively, and responsive.

🐾 *Above: A distinctively shaded caramel Tonkinese. During the 1960s, these cats were known as Golden Siamese because of their warm coloration.*

Temperament: Like the Siamese, the Tonkinese loves company and dislikes being left alone for long periods. Owners who are absent for much of the day should consider acquiring two cats to keep each other company. Chances are excellent that both will be lively, intelligent, and an asset to the household.

Special Characteristics: These cats are very clever at finding ways to escape from the house or apartment, so special attention should be paid to "security" measures before introducing a Tonkinese to the household and when a move is planned.

Origins: In a sense, the Tonkinese is a reinvented breed that occurs naturally in its countries of origin, Myanmar (formerly Burma) and Thailand (formerly Siam). A single Canadian breeder set out to develop a cat with the most attractive features of both the Siamese and the Burmese, with outstanding results. The Tonkinese was first accepted for championship competition by the Canadian Cat Association in 1965.

🐾 A cream Tonkinese kitten (left) is one of the many self-colored varieties acceptable for showing under GCCF standards.

The Rex Group

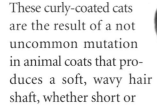

These curly-coated cats are the result of a not uncommon mutation in animal coats that produces a soft, wavy hair shaft, whether short or

Appearance: The *Cornish Rex* has a short, silky coat in which the fur lies close to the body, falling in waves like the fleece of a Persian lamb. Its body type is slim and elongated, almost like that of a whippet, and it now comes in colors ranging from calico to blue mackerel tabby, black smoke, and red classic tabby.

Feline Facts

🐾 Research has shown that all four of the different Rex breeds carry different recessive genes that result in the distinctively curly coats.

🐾 *At left, a lovely tortie Cornish Rex, showing the breed's long, slender body type, and fleecy, curly coat.*

🐾 *Above, a strikingly marked seal point and white Cornish Rex.*

long. This mutation has appeared in several places since the first (Cornish) Rex appeared in a litter in Cornwall, England (1950), and was so called for its resemblance to the Rex rabbit. At this writing, four other types of curly-coated cats have been recognized as breeds, including the Devon Rex, German Rex, Selkirk Rex, and the relatively new long-haired American breed called the LaPerm.

🐾 *This red cream Cornish Rex displays the curly whiskers that are unique to the Rex breeds.*

Across the water, two new mutations occurred during the 1980s, resulting in the *Selkirk Rex* and the *LaPerm*—the CFA's most recently recognized breed. The original Selkirk Rex was born to a farm cat in Wyoming's Selkirk Mountains, sporting a soft, full, curly coat that felt like lambswool. Since then, both short- and long-haired varieties have been developed, and all colors and patterns are acceptable for showing.

The LaPerm originated with an Oregon farm kitten that had a long-haired coat forming curly ringlets all over its body. (Curiously, the LaPerm will usually lose all its fur during kittenhood; when the new coat grows in, it is much curlier than before. Even the whiskers and eyebrows are curly!)

This breed, like its counterparts, now includes a wide variety of coat colors and patterns, including vibrant reds and bicolors.

The body types of both the American breeds differ widely from those of the British Rexes. The Selkirk Rex is a large, heavy-boned

🐾 *In the black smoke Cornish Rex (right), dark coloration is restricted to the awn hairs (coarser secondary hairs) and the down is silver.*

The *Devon Rex*, too, originated with a single kitten, this one born in Devon, England (1960), with a curly coat from a different mutant gene. The coat presents a rippled effect rather than a tightly waved appearance. The Devon has strikingly large ears on a small head, an elfin expression enhanced by large oval eyes, and a slim Siamese-type body. It now comes in every conceivable color and pattern.

The *German Rex* originated in Berlin with a curly-coated black cat named Lämmchen ("little lamb") in the early 1950s. It was first recognized as a separate breed in 1956.

☙ *Its large, pointed ears and dramatic eyes give the Devon Rex something of an elfin appearance. At left, a silver tabby. Note the rippled appearance of the wavy coat.*

Behavior: All of the relatively recent curly-coated breeds have received high marks for their adaptability, intelligence, and playfulness. The Cornish Rex has been described as "a born acrobat" and the Devon Rex as "almost impossible to resist." The American breeds are cited for devotion to their families and the robust health and longevity resulting from their sturdy ancestry.

cat with a straight back and a muscular torso. The standard calls for shoulders and hips of the same width, and the head is round, broad, and full-cheeked. The LaPerm is a medium-bodied cat of the type known as semiforeign (slightly elongated). Its triangular face, tufted ears, and wide-eyed expression add to its appeal.

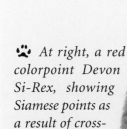
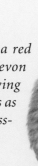

☙ *At right, a red colorpoint Devon Si-Rex, showing Siamese points as a result of cross-breeding.*

🐾 *This black German Rex shows the well-arched back and muscular hindquarters that make it capable of high jumps and amazing speed. Interest in this breed is growing steadily.*

Temperament: As a group, the Rexes are described as home-loving, nontemperamental, and eager to please. They are not especially vocal or demanding.

Special Characteristics: Surprisingly, most of the rexed cat breeds do not require extensive grooming and shed little. The LaPerm cat, for example, like the Poodle, catches shed hair in its curls and rarely transfers it to the environment.

Origins: See above.

🐾 *The German Rex ticked tabby at left displays the long, tapering tail that is a standard for its breed.*

93

Sphynx

Hairless cats are the result of a spontaneous genetic mutation that has occurred several times that we know of during the past century. In fact, the Sphynx is not truly hairless: Its body is covered with a light coat of fine down that is almost invisible. It feels like chamois to the touch. These cats are both playful and affectionate, and Sphynx owners swear by them, but many people are put off by their appearance. To this date, the breed is very rare outside the United States and has been accepted by only two associations—the American Cat Association and the International Cat Association.

Appearance: The Sphynx has a medium-length body that is sturdy and rounded and a long, slender neck. The broad chest is barrel-shaped and the triangular head has prominent cheekbones and large eyes that slant up to the outer edge of the ears, which are very large and upright. The long, tapered tail feels hard to the touch. For show purposes, the Sphynx can be any color and pattern, including colorpoint, and it has been suggested that because of the invisibility of its hair, the pattern and color seem almost to be tattooed on the skin. The hair on the points is short, soft, and tightly packed.

Behavior: The Sphynx is active and affectionate, but it must always be kept indoors. It cannot tolerate exposure to direct sunlight.

Temperament: This is a very gentle breed, and its inquisitive, pixielike face has great charm. It seems to be contented with itself and everyone around it.

🐾 *The nearly hairless Sphynx may be any color or pattern (at right, a chocolate tabby), but it will never lack for attention because its appearance is so distinctive, from its unusual coat to its prominent ears.*

Special Characteristics: The Sphynx is unique in several ways. Unlike most other cats, it sweats, and it should be sponged daily with a warm, damp sponge to remove oils from the skin. The skin often has a wrinkled appearance, especially in kittens, because of the lack of an insulating coat, and the nose is covered with velvety fur in keeping with the point colors.

Origins: During the early 1900s, a cat resembling today's breed was exhibited as the New Mexican Hairless. In the 1970s, cats of similar appearance were born in Ontario, Canada, and efforts to gain recognition for the breed began. Another spontaneous mutation occurred in Minnesota during the 1970s, and most of the Sphynx cats registered today descend from these hairless kittens.

Peterbald

Like the Sphynx, the Russian-born Peterbald appears to be hairless, but has a very fine down coat along its body, which feels like soft chamois, and more fur on the ears, muzzle, tail, and feet. This new breed, which appeared in 1994, has the Oriental's graceful, slim body type and wedge-shaped head.

🐾 *Left: A seal male Peterbald shows the lean, sleek body type of this new Russian breed, which was named for its city of origin, St. Petersburg.*

Feline Facts

🐾 Like the Sphynx, the Peterbald has a wedge-shaped head, very large ears, and a wrinkled appearance as a result of its semihairlessness.

Appearance: The Peterbald differs from the Sphynx in appearing very lean and sleek, while the Sphynx has a round, full abdomen. The Peterbald's body is cylindrical and finely boned. Its ears are very large, broad at the base and set high on the head. Eye color is usually green-gold, but as new colors—based on the skin pigment—continue to appear, pointed and white cats may have blue eyes. The cat's skin is thin and wrinkled, and it has long, slim legs and a long, tapering tail. Breeders recommend that the Peterbald be bathed about once a month and towel dried.

🐾 *A brush chocolate female with championship potential.*

Behavior: Owners and breeders have described the Peterbald as loving, friendly, and affectionate, eager to receive attention and to play. They get along well with all members of the household, including dogs and other cats.

Temperament: These cats tend to pine when left alone all day, since they are extremely companionable and outgoing, so it can be a good idea to adopt two littermates.

Special Characteristics: The Peterbald's graceful body is seen to full advantage due to its relative hairlessness. It received championship status in Russian associations soon after it appeared in a breeding program at St. Petersburg.

Origins: The first known ancestor of the Peterbald was a blue tortie cat named Varya, who had a hairlessness gene that was unrelated to that of the Sphynx. Her first kittens were born in 1989 in St. Petersburg, Russia.

Japanese Bobtail

Behavior: This is an intelligent and active cat that needs a warm, indoor climate and thrives on interaction with people. Its manner is vivacious, and it usually responds in a soft voice when spoken to.

Feline Facts

🐾 Japanese legend holds that the image of a *maneki neko* (beckoning cat) brings the viewer luck, good fortune, and happiness.

This is an ancient and rare breed that is indigenous to Japan and most of Southeast Asia.

Distinguished by its unusual short tail, ideally carried upright like a pom-pom, this cat also has long hindquarters designed for running and leaping and is extremely active. It was unknown in the United States until 1968, when three short-haired animals were imported from Japan. During the 1970s, breed standards were agreed and the Bobtail was granted championship status as a shorthair in 1976. In 1993 the long-haired Japanese Bobtail was accepted for showing.

Appearance: This is a medium-sized cat with lean, elegant lines and a long, finely shaped head with high cheekbones. Large, oval eyes are wide set, and the ears are large and upright, with rounded tips. The long, slender hind legs are naturally bent when the Bobtail is standing in a relaxed posture. The coat is soft, silky, and flat, with minimal shedding. The breed standard makes a ruff desirable, as well as ear and toe tufts. This cat comes in all colors except solid lilac, chocolate, and colorpointed.

🐾 *At top, a tortie and white Japanese Bobtail; at right, the popular black and white with the requisite pompom-type tail.*

Temperament: The Japanese Bobtail is friendly by nature, highly adaptable, and extremely good with children.

Special Characteristics: This cat's unusual tail may be flexible or rigid, but it must be clearly visible and include one or more curves, angles, or kinks. The Japanese prefer bright coats in these cats, especially calico (called *mi-ke*).

Origins: The Japanese Bobtail's origins are shrouded in antiquity, but its lean conformation and agility in running and leaping suggests that its forebears included wild cats of Southeast Asia.

Manx

The unique tailless Manx breed originated on the Isle of Man in the Irish Sea. It became the subject of Celtic legend, which tells of warriors who attached cat tails to their helmets for success in battle. Thus mother cats began giving birth to tailless kittens to save them. The far likelier account is that the Manx gene is a spon-

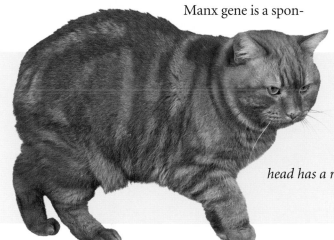

taneous mutation that appeared on the Isle of Man and spread rapidly through its resident cat population.

In behavior and temperament, the Manx may be cautious around strangers, but it is a good-natured pet that enjoys interacting with its family. It likes to leap to the highest available perch, and shows intelligence, curiosity, and playfulness. It has a soft voice with a quiet trill and does well with dogs and children if introduced at an early age.

One unusual trait is the Manx tendency to collect or retrieve small objects, and even to bury them, as a dog does. These cats are generally hardy and healthy, sometimes reaching the age of twenty years.

😺 *At right, the distinctive silver spotted Manx. This breed has a long-haired cousin called the Cymric (pronounced Kim'rik)—the Celtic name for Welsh, as the Isle of Man is midway between the coasts of Ireland, England, and Wales.*

Special Characteristics: Show specimens, called Rumpies, have no tail vertebrae whatever, but these are rare. Both Manx and Cymric breeders divide pet-quality kittens according to the size of the vestigial tail into "Stumpies" and "Longies." Long-haired cats are judged as a Manx division in some U.S. associations and as the Cymric breed in others.

😺 *This handsome red tabby Manx is representative of the breed: a small but powerfully built cat with a deep, broad chest. Its long hind legs cause its back to form a perfectly round rump. The broad head has a round muzzle and small ears set wide apart.*

Although the Manx was a well-known breed in Britain before the 1870s, it is no longer accepted in shows sponsored there, on ground that breeding this cat will perpetuate a lethal spine defect.

Origins: See above.

Cat Identifier

Centuries of random breeding have resulted in millions of domestic cats—the ones that most of us own and love. They differ in body shape and size and show countless coat colors and patterns; eye colors and shapes; long, short, or medium-length fur; and fur quality ranging from fine and silky to short and dense. It is from these many types of cats, and a number of spontaneous mutations thereof, that most of our pedigree cats have been selectively crossbred to produce the purebred varieties that appear in the previous pages.

The impetus toward producing domestic cats in different breeds and varieties came from the first Official Cat Show, held in 1871 in London's splendid Crystal Palace. The revered Queen Victoria was a dedicated animal lover, and many members of society began to acquire and breed pedigree cats, which became a kind of status symbol.

At this first show, most of the cats exhibited were shorthairs. They included tortoiseshells (later called "torties"), tortoiseshell and whites, a handful of Siamese with black rather than brown points, some tailless Manx, and self- or solid-colored blues. Several Persians, called Longhairs or Eastern cats, were also shown. Over time, they became so popular that the more familiar domestic cats lost ground in popularity. Then the Persians, in turn, were outshone by the Siamese, and so it went. Here we will see how nonpedigree cats from many different backgrounds show the various qualities described above that are now used to set standards for the many pedigree varieties.

Fur Colors: Solid (Self) Colors

If your cat has no visible markings on a solid-color coat, for example, black or brownish-black, it is a solid, or, especially in the UK, a self-colored cat. A solid blue is blue-gray all over, ranging from a dark slate color to medium gray or a pale ash color. A solid white, similarly, is white all over, sometimes with blue eyes, in other cases with green or gold eyes, or odd eyes as previously mentioned—one eye is blue and the other is green or gold.

Diluted colors refer to a paler version of a basic color; for example, dilute black gives blue, and dilute chocolate gives lilac. This term is used mainly by breeders familiar with genetics, who know that the presence of the mutant gene "d" reduces the strength of a particular color. If the colors being diluted exist as a pattern—say, calico—the cat's markings will appear as blue and cream on a white ground, rather than the usual patches of black, red, and white. (Note that cat fanciers use the word "red" for the color that is more widely called orange, or ginger. They also use the term "blue" for the color that most of us would refer to as gray.)

A cat with a reddish-brown coat is called cinnamon, or sorrel. There are at least ten variants on this color, ranging from cinnamon shaded to the delicate pinkish-cream coat known as fawn.

🐾 *Top: A Burmese solid chocolate, with the dilute color variant, lilac, at right.*

🐾 Above: A solid cinnamon-colored cat, with its dilute fur-color counterpart, a fawn, at right.
Below: A black-coated Angora, with the dilute color, blue, at right.

Fur Colors: Nonsolid Colors

Shaded and Tipped Fur: A shaded coat is made up of relatively pale hairs that have a darker tip appearing a moderate distance down the length of the hair. A tipped coat is similar, but the darker color begins closer to the end of the hair. In this case, the cat appears light in color, with just a hint of the color of the hair tips.

🐾 *At top, a tipped coat on a Himalayan, which appears light in color on the body, but shows a hint of the darker hair ends. At right, a Turkish Angora has been bred in a caramel shaded variety. (The term "caramel" is used differently by several of the major cat associations. It may refer either to a reddish-brown coat, a bluish-fawn coat, or any degree of shading on either of these colors.)*

Smoke Fur: The CFA publishes a fact sheet on common cat colors that loosely defines a smoke cat as one with white roots at the hair of a solid color like black or grey. This type of coat can appear in purpose-bred pedigree cats or in random-bred nonpedigrees, but it is likelier to observe it in cats bred to this standard. The GCCF describes a black smoke, for example, as "a cat of contrasts, the undercolour being as ash-white as possible, with the tips shading to black, the dark points being most defined on the back, head and feet, and the light points on frill, flanks and ear-tufts." A very attractive feature of the smoke is that it appears to change color when it's active, and the pale undercoat ripples into visibility.

🐾 *A smoke coat is illustrated in the cat at right, while the coat at left is ticked.*

Ticked Fur: The coat pattern described as ticked refers to the fact that each hair is banded with alternate rings of light and dark, like the fur of a squirrel. Also called agouti, a cat of this description often has a tabby coat pattern, with thin pencil lines on the face and a tabby "M" on the forehead, varying in depth from almost invisible to quite distinct.

🐾 *Right: Another example of a ticked coat.*

Coat Patterns: Parti-Color and Bicolor

A parti-color cat has one or more colors and patterns with white, while a bicolor is about half white with a number of other markings on various areas of the body. The key to describing cats with white markings is the relative areas of white color. For example, a cat with white paws only is described as "mitted," while a harlequin is mostly white with several patches of color. Your cat may be a black-and-white with white paws, chest, and belly (informally called a "tuxedo cat") or a cream tabby and white. Any color with clear white markings (as opposed to shaded points, often seen in the Siamese) can be defined as either a parti-color or a bicolor.

🐾 *This handsome long-haired cat has a parti-color coat.*

Coat Patterns: Colorpoints

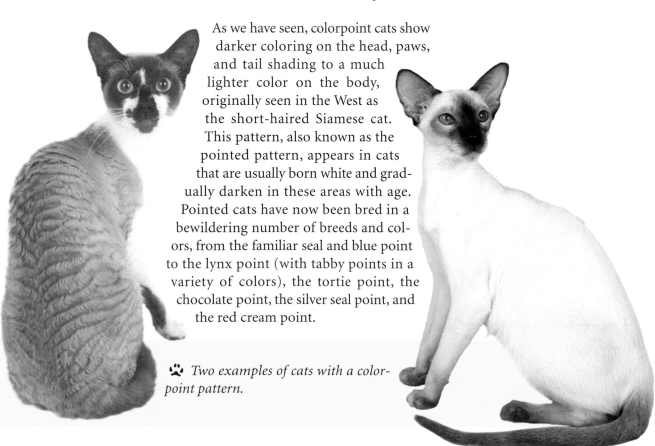

As we have seen, colorpoint cats show darker coloring on the head, paws, and tail shading to a much lighter color on the body, originally seen in the West as the short-haired Siamese cat. This pattern, also known as the pointed pattern, appears in cats that are usually born white and gradually darken in these areas with age. Pointed cats have now been bred in a bewildering number of breeds and colors, from the familiar seal and blue point to the lynx point (with tabby points in a variety of colors), the tortie point, the chocolate point, the silver seal point, and the red cream point.

🐾 *Two examples of cats with a color-point pattern.*

Coat Patterns: Tortoiseshell

These cats are randomly patched all over with red, black, and cream. They appear in both short- and long-haired varieties, and often show a blaze of one of these colors on the forehead or nose. The dilute tortoise-shell is a blue and cream color, and tortoiseshells with white markings are described as "tortie and whites." Male tortoiseshells are very rare, and those that do appear are usually sterile.

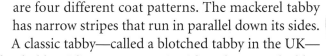

Above and right: Two torties. Below: Tabby patterns illustrated in two purebred cats.

Coat Patterns: Tabby

The striped tabby, or tiger cat, is probably the most familiar—and the original—domestic cat, as descended from wild ancestors whose coats provided camouflage in their jungle and savanna habitats. All tabbies have the three-banded agouti hair shaft, but there are four different coat patterns. The mackerel tabby has narrow stripes that run in parallel down its sides. A classic tabby—called a blotched tabby in the UK—has bold, swirling patterns on its sides. The spotted tabby has spots all over its sides—sometimes large, sometimes small—while the ticked tabby, described on page 103, shows neither distinct spots nor stripes, but has tabby markings on the face. Color varieties vary enormously, from a light-gray ground color to a rich orange color.

Body Shapes

The cat's structural appearance is closely related to its place of origin, whether warm, cold or temperate; the work it was expected to perform (most notably, rodent control); and the selective breeding for type that has taken place over the years.

Animals like the Norwegian Forest Cat and the Maine Coon have proportionately large, sturdy bodies and dense fur to cope with the cold climates in which they developed. Breeds like the domestic shorthair, whether American, British, or European, tend to have rather smaller bodies that are rounded and set low on the legs—the type described as "cobby." Originally, these were working cats of Western Europe: like their Egyptian and Roman ancestors, they performed valuable service in controlling mice and rats in the farmyard, the granary, the city, and aboard ships, which ensured their widespread distribution.

 *Long-haired cats sometimes appear considerably more slender when their fur is wet; their body shapes are not always obvious under their copious coats. A short-haired cat, however, is readily identifiable as slender, medium-built, large, or cobby in shape.*

Body types described as slender, or "foreign," are associated with breeds like the Siamese, which have long, slim bodies and angular, wedge-shaped heads with very large ears. Originally, they lived a privileged life in temples and palaces, and were presented only to important dignitaries, some of whom brought these fascinating cats to the West, where they were crossbred to produce a variety of new breeds, both long- and short-haired. Some of these breeds are variously known as Asians and Orientals, as described in the previous pages.

With the growth of the cat fancy, standards have been set for every breed, including specific requirements as to head, ears, eyes, body, coat, colors, and other characteristics. These standards vary from one major organization to another, and sometimes the same breed is known by different names, but they ensure that a recognized breed will conform to certain requirements that will perpetuate its most desirable qualities. TICA standards for the Abyssinian, for example, award 30 points for the head, 10 for coat texture, 35 for the body, and 25 for color and pattern.

If your cat is a nonpedigree, you can still recognize its basic body type as cobby, semicobby, slender, Asian, and so forth. The United States has recognized no fewer than thirty-five breeds, some of which are widely known, while Britain has sixteen recognized breeds at this writing.

🐾 *The cats on this page are all slender in shape, ultimately descended from cats that originated in the East—though they have long been popular in Western countries too.*

Facial Shapes

The face is unmistakable as a clue to a given cat's ancestry. Round-faced cats include the extremely popular Persian, or Longhair, and the familiar domestic shorthair—now the most popular of all household pets.

🐾 *Left and below: Round-faced cats. The example at left has the "flattened" face typical of Persians.*

🐾 *Above and right: A cat with an angular face that broadens from a narrow muzzle to large, widely spaced ears is of Siamese or other Oriental ancestry, whether or not it is a pedigree.*

Ear Shapes

Ear size and placement varies widely from one breed to another, and among random-bred cats, depending upon their body type and ancestry. We are probably most familiar with the medium-size, pointed ears of the many strains of domestic shorthairs, which are set on either side of a rounded head. Less familiar is the curled ear on cats like the American Curl, and the appealing folded-forward ear of the Scottish fold, both of which occurred originally as the result of spontaneous mutations. The Persian Longhair and the Exotic Shorthair have noticeably small, tufted ears, while the nearly hairless Sphynx has comparatively huge ears flaring out on either side of an angular Oriental-type face (critics have compared them to bat wings!). The Siamese has large ears set well apart and of the same color as the mask, legs, and tail.

🐾 *Ear types, clockwise from top left: large, batlike pointed ears on a Sphynx; relatively large, pointed ears; folded, or curl, ears; and the small-sized ears most commonly seen in cats of Western origin.*

Eye Shapes

Round eyes in a comparatively round face are typical of pedigree cats including the Norwegian Forest Cat, the Birman, and the Korat, and of most nonpedigree cats as well. They give the face an appealing expression, and, more importantly, allow the average cat to enjoy a much wider vision field than we do. Like all felines, they have pupils that expand and contract according to available light, which enables them to see well in very dim light—a vital ability in an animal born to hunt. However, the idea that cats can see in total darkness is a myth.

🐾 *Three examples of cats with round eyes.*

Almond-shaped or other types of slanted eyes are typical of the long, slender Oriental breeds and the new breeds that have been developed from them, including the Balinese and the Peterbald, which appears to have extremely slanted eyes because of its decidedly wedge-shaped face and very large pointed ears. Eye colors vary considerably according to the light (which is why cats' eyes appear to glow in the dark), but standards have emerged for the various breeds, often compatible with coat color. The average nonpedigree cat appears to have yellow eyes, ranging from chartreuse yellow to gold and amber. The Siamese has striking deep-blue eyes, while the Havana has vivid green eyes and the Egyptian Mau has eyes of a light gooseberry-green color.

🐾 *Three examples of cats with almond-shaped or slanted eyes.*

2

Are You Ready For Your Feline Friend?

Since responsible pet ownership entails a lifetime commitment, it's important to know that pets acquired on impulse often don't work out. In many cases, the idea of getting a kitten or even a grown cat is fairly idealized. "Won't it be nice to have 'someone' around who's always glad to see me, loves to purr on my lap, and is content just to be around me?" The responsibilities involved are either unknown or minimized—until reality sets in, and one finds that the business of having a pet is not just a matter of sentiment. It involves a fellow creature that is as dependent upon you as a child, having long since exchanged its "wild and free" status for the company and protection of humans.

Timing: Yes or No?

Cats have an undeserved reputation for being aloof and self-sufficient. On the contrary, they are very sociable animals and have certain emotional needs that must be respected if a mutual bond is to flourish. If, for example, you are planning to move into a new home in the near future, it would be unwise to acquire a new pet before doing so. Like all animals (ourselves included), a kitten or cat needs gradual introduction to a new environment and time to establish itself in a

> 🐾 A cat can be a wonderful companion, but you'll need to make adjustments before you take on the responsibilities of pet ownership.

safe, caring atmosphere. Similarly, if you are making a major life decision involving marriage, a new job, or the birth of a baby, it would probably be as well to postpone introducing a pet until you have had time to adjust to these changes yourself.

Are You Prepared for the Mess?

Granted, cats don't have to be walked every day like dogs, but they do have preferences that will make themselves known. For example, if you're squeamish about things like cleaning the litter box every day or reluctant to scrub food and water bowls, wipe down feeding mats, and dehair cat beds and other accessories, you might want to consider the following checklist of "Human Habits That Drive Cats Crazy" by Arden Moore, in the February 2002 issue of *Cat Fancy*:

Human Habits That Drive Cats Crazy

1. Blaring music
2. People tossing and turning in bed
3. Yelling and raising your voice
4. Superstressed people (They sense this more readily than one would believe.)
5. Dirty litter boxes
6. Tardy feedings
7. Carrier, car, clinic
8. Ill-mannered children
9. Adopting another cat or dog
10. Forced affection

Cost and Effect

As pointed out in the following chapter, even if you adopt a cat from a shelter or from a friend's litter, it will require an initial expenditure on a variety of accessories to meet your new pet's needs. There will also be ongoing costs in terms of spaying or neutering, food, veterinary examinations, annual vaccinations, and, in case of illness or injury, any medications or surgery your cat might need. Once you have bonded with an animal, its well-being will be paramount with you and there may be sacrifices involved in maintaining your commitment in the face of unexpected adverse events.

If you decide to purchase a pedigreed cat both the initial expense and the ongoing costs will be higher than those of a nonpedigree—especially if you want a show-quality animal, with all the attendant costs of travel, grooming, registration fees, association memberships, and so forth. However, many owners have found these activities so rewarding that they have become an avocation for them and their pets. It depends on whether you have, or can make, the time to become a full-fledged cat fancier, or even a breeder in your own right—and whether your pet responds positively to these experiences.

Love and Attention

There are no price tags on these intangible qualities, but they are the sum and substance of your relationship with your feline friend. We have all seen miracles of healing performed on even the shyest shelter cat or anxious stray that has blossomed in a caring environment, becoming an invaluable source of satisfaction and enjoyment to its gratified owners. The cat with the loftiest pedigree also needs your love and attention to thrive. If you have a job that keeps you away from home most of the day or entails extensive travel, your cat will be lonely, whether in an expensive kennel or at home with a neighbor coming by to care for it once or twice a day. Pet ownership should probably be postponed in such cases until your life is more home-centered.

Paws for Thought

🐾 It is never a good idea to give pets as a gift.

This may well be the place to mention that one should never give a pet as a gift unless one is certain that the proposed recipient is ready and eager to assume that responsibility. A pet is not a toy for children or grownups. Too many of these well-meant gifts are eventually abandoned or end up in a cage at the local humane society. And the effects of neglect, in the long run, can be as damaging as outright abuse. Fortunately, some enlightened shelter officials are now recognizing the need for socialization of timid cats or kittens and recruiting trained volunteers to provide foster care in home environments.

As former ASPCA president Roger Karas points out in the foreword to *Adopting Cats and Kittens* by Connie Jankowski: "A badly placed animal moves from one home to the next, from one generation to the next, back and forth, until it is nearly wild with anxiety, uncertainty, and insecurity. At that point, it is probably useless as a pet and will eventually be euthanized, if it is not killed by a car or a truck or disease." Sad, but these are the facts of the matter, which are only too clear to people who care about animals.

A cat, unlike a Golden Retriever, can make a life in a relatively small space, but you'll want to be sure that your housing provides enough room for your new pet to play and exercise without feeling cramped. Kittens and young cats need more room to spread out than the older animal, who is more sedate and settled in her habits.

> *"The really great thing about cats is their endless variety. One can pick a cat to fit almost any kind of décor, color scheme, income, personality, mood. But under the fur, whatever color it may be, there still lies, essentially unchanged, one of the world's free souls."*
> —Eric Gurney

Almost all felines spend two-thirds of their time sleeping, but there is a much wider range of activity among younger cats whose playtime develops the strengths and skills inherent in their ancestry and helps to develop a well-rounded personality.

🐾 *If you're preparing for the birth of a baby or planning to move house in the near future, this isn't the right time to bring home a new pet. You'll need to be able to provide a settled environment and find time to give your kitty lots of attention to help him become a happy member of your household.*

Are You Ready and Willing?

🐾 Consider the size and placement of the litter box/es.

🐾 You will need to clean the litter box daily.

🐾 You will need ample time for bonding with your new cat or kitten.

🐾 Storage space is needed for its toys, grooming tools, and other accessories.

🐾 A well-made cat bed is essential, with a liner that is easily removed for laundering.

🐾 Research with your vet the best food/s for your new pet.

Warning: Good nutrition will not include table scraps; raw meat, fish, or poultry; bones of any kind; chocolate (contains theobromine: a small amount can be fatal); alcohol in any form; or raw egg white. See Chapter 6 for more information on basic nutrition—not a matter on which to economize.

🐾 You'll need to clean up occasional messes caused by hair balls and overeating.

🐾 You will probably need a supply of lint rollers or similar hair removers to keep your clothes (especially dark ones) and your upholstery free of fur.

Your Circumstances at Home

Before you acquire a cat, you should consider whether your home is suitable and whether your household can accommodate a new pet.

Do You Live in a House with a Garden?

If so, you will decide which, if any, rooms will be off-limits to your cat and whether your garden can serve as a protective enclosure where you can enjoy outdoor activities with her. In the absence of a walled or otherwise secure outdoor space, you may decide to provide a sheltered cat run.

A good idea was suggested to *Cat Fancy* readers (February 2002) by Kris Bender, whose son had out-

grown his play area, complete with sandbox, slides, treehouse, and swing. With some extra hardware, lumber, and her husband's help, Bender created a luxury run for the couple's four cats that included a weatherproof enclosure for cold winter days and unrestricted access to the spacious upper level.

Are You an Apartment Dweller?

Obviously, your first order of business is to find out whether your apartment or condominium complex allows pets, and if so, what kind. Many apartments have a "no pets" clause in their leases; others will allow pets of specified weights and sizes with payment of a security deposit.

As a prospective cat owner, you will probably have few problems with the latter type of housing, since dogs—rightly or wrongly—are often deemed "more trouble."

Many cats spend their lives happily in small to moderate-sized apartments, especially if they have never had the experience of being outdoors. They enjoy watching birds, other animals, and people from the windows, but be sure that your new pet doesn't escape from the apartment when a visitor comes inside. Chances are the cat will panic once she is on unfamiliar turf, either bolting through the halls or darting outside. My family once moved my mother from one floor of her apartment house to another, and her cat seemingly disappeared

🐾 *Indoor cats while away many happy hours at the window, watching the world go by. They'll be perfectly content to stay in if they've never had the experience of being outdoors. You should take care to provide ample opportunity for indoor cats to exercise and entertain themselves with suitable toys and diversions.*

during the course of the day. We all hunted through the halls calling for Charley and finally found him—wedged under the shoe rack at the back of her closet. He was extremely put out by all the disruption and let us know it by voting with all four feet.

Paws for Thought

🐾 Cats love to climb, experiment with their claws by playing with fabrics, and curl up on your furniture and clothing. They can be trained to some extent and kept out of certain rooms in the house, but you should ask yourself how much you'd mind the extra housework and occasional damage to furnishings and clothing before you decide to become a cat owner.

What About Children?

If you have children, they will almost certainly be ecstatic at the prospect of having a pet, and rightly so. Many of us remember our childhood pets as a wonderful part of our early lives. However, there are guidelines that will help ease the new cat or kitten into your home situation.

The first is to let the children know that the newcomer needs time to get used to all of you. Don't rush up on him all at once, and always approach him from the front—don't scoop him up from behind without warning. This will scare him and make him want to run and hide.

Teach children how to pick a cat up so that it's safe and comfortable and to handle him gently at all times. A responsible child can be entrusted with his feeding, but don't allow children to feed him treats that may be bad for his health.

While the cat is becoming acclimated to the household, you can show the children how to pick him up and get him used to *gentle* handling. Put one hand under his chest, just behind his forelegs, and the other hand under his stomach, in front of his hind legs. Lift him up carefully and hold him for a short time in a comfortable position, fully supporting his hindquarters with your hand. Emphasize the need to hold the cat securely, but not to squeeze him, and to put him down again before he starts squirming to get away. Never let him jump from your arms, as this could cause injury.

If you demonstrate this technique a few times a day, the new pet will begin to build trust, and

Paws for Thought

If you have infants or toddlers in your household, consider whether this is the right time to acquire a cat. Do you have space to keep a cat and small children apart whenever you're not able to supervise them closely? (This might involve putting your cat outside.) Your children should be old enough to understand how to respect a cat and not to hurt it, whether through excessive exuberance or a bad temper. If a cat feels threatened or afraid, it will defend itself by fleeing or, if necessary, lashing out.

the children will have a better idea of how to further that process. Even toddlers can benefit from these demonstrations, but be sure not to leave them unsupervised with the new cat or kitten. Their tendency is to "grab and hug" or "grab and carry"—usually upside down.

It is also advisable not to let the children feed the cat anything that they might consider a "treat." In fact, only the most responsible child should be shown how to prepare the cat's regular food and entrusted with giving it meals and fresh water in a timely manner. You had best take care of this yourself if the child finds the job burdensome or proves unreliable in meeting the pet's needs.

What About Other Pets?

The chapter "Bringing Kitty Home" describes the process of introducing the newcomer to a multicat household. Obviously, other pets like birds, hamsters, rabbits, and guinea pigs should be securely housed in their own pens or cages so Fluffy can't act out on her impulses to see them as prey. Introducing a dog has a protocol all its own.

As with all animal introductions, scent is the all-important factor. Before letting cat and dog have visual contact, let them sniff each other's bedding. Your dog should know and obey those basic commands to "sit" and "stay," even in the presence of a new animal. You can reinforce compliance with food treats and praise.

🐾 *If you have a goldfish or a rabbit, you'll need to keep them safe from your new cat. Unless cats grow up together, they won't easily bond with each other.*

"Cats have a lot to say, though not very much of it is complimentary. Mrow . . . you're late with the food. Mrow . . . why haven't you opened the curtains yet? Mrow . . . how come I can't go outside today? A happy cat is a silent cat."
—Michael J. Rosen

Some authorities recommend having another family member bring the new cat into the room and sit quietly with her on his lap while you hold the dog on a leash at a distance. Dogs who have grown up with cats will be eager to chase and play with the newcomer, but these tendencies need to be curbed until the cat feels secure in the dog's presence. Continue controlled and supervised contact until you're sure they are becoming friendly, and don't leave them alone together for some weeks while you're out of the house. In most cases, an alliance will develop and you'll come home to *both* of them sleeping on your bed.

🐾 *Cats and dogs can become the best of friends, but this blissful state of affairs is achieved more quickly if you're thoughtful about their introductions. These scenarios (right and below) could be your cat's worst nightmare!*

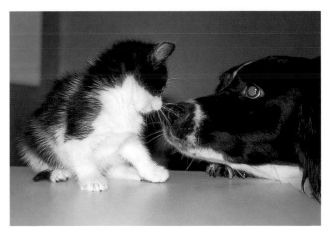

Ready, Set, Go for a Kitty?

1. Do you really yearn for a furry, purry, lifelong loving companion to brighten your days?

2. How many hours do you spend at home each day? Are you at home on weekends, or often absent from home? Cats need a secure bond with their owners or families for their basic well-being.

3. How is your vacation schedule? Two to four weeks away from home each year will require a professional pet sitter, a faithful friend to stay with your furbaby, or a reputable kennel or breeder with which to board her.

4. Can you afford a cat? Even a nonpedigree kitten can cost between $500 and $1,000 in vet bills, supplies, etc., during its first year.

5. Do you have the patience to see a rambunctious kitten through to maturity, or would you rather start with a more sedate, full-grown cat in need of a loving home?

6. Do your family members or any of your regular visitors have any allergies or suffer from ailurophobia—extreme fear of cats?

7. Do you object to cleaning the litter box daily?

8. Can you commit to allowing your cat outdoors only in a safe, well-secured environment? Otherwise, he poses a threat to birds and other wildlife and is at risk himself from traffic, fighting, pesticides, and other hazards.

9. Will you be able to groom your cat regularly to maintain her health and appearance?

10. Are you willing to have your cat spayed or neutered at the appropriate time, unless you plan to breed or show your pet as an unaltered ("whole") male or female?

Indoors or Out?

This basic question has everything to do with your cat's health, safety, and longevity. In former times, the question almost never arose. Barn cats were "working" cats who kept the barn free of rodents, slept there, and

were given an occasional meal of table scraps. House cats were usually let in and out of doors at will in the belief that they could take care of themselves and would wend their way home for food and shelter when they were ready. The facts of contemporary life have led many animal caregivers to reassess this matter of indoor versus outdoor cats.

*"I situate myself, and seat myself,
And where you recline I shall recline,
For every armchair belonging to you as good as
belongs to me.*

*I loaf and curl up my tail,
I yawn and loaf at my ease after rolling in the
catnip patch.*

*   *   *

*You can never know where I am or what I am,
But I am good company to you nonetheless,
And really do regret I broke your inkwell.*

*Failing to find me at first keep looking,
Missing me one place search another,
I sit up here waiting for you to come and carry me
down."*

—James Beard, *Poetry for Cats*

As rural communities dwindle in size and population density increases, especially around our larger cities, "the great outdoors" poses growing dangers to cats, which, in turn, pose certain threats to the environment, especially in their destruction of birds. Each year, more veterinarians are recommending the indoor life for cats, or outdoor exposure only in a controlled environment like a secure cat run. The checklist of potential hazards to the outdoor cat continues to grow:

- Motor vehicles
- Fights with other animals
- Disease-carrying rodents
- Rabies
- Trees, where cats can get stuck
- Accidental poisoning from chemicals, pesticides, or rotting food
- Indiscriminate mating by cats that have not been sterilized
- Theft, especially in the case of a pedigreed cat
  - Cats getting lost
  - Exposure to diseases and parasites
  - Deliberate cruelty

All this makes a convincing case for keeping your cat indoors or leash-training him (see the following chapter) so you can make outings together, whether in the garden or to a nearby park or woodland.

Feline Facts

🐾 According to the Tufts University School of Veterinary Medicine, as published in their magazine Catnip (March 2003), bringing out the best in your indoor cat asks you to "Think like a feline and ask yourself, what would make an ordinary house into a dream home? Providing the right litter box and the right scratching post in the right locations can eliminate many behavioral problems. That's the message delivered at the 2002 Tufts Animal Expo in Boston by Suzanne Hetts, Ph.D., a certified applied animal behaviorist. 'Two of the most prized possessions for a cat are a litter box and a scratching post,' says Dr. Hetts. 'Clawing the furniture, missing the litter box and other problems can often be resolved by offering cat-friendly litter boxes and places to sharpen their claws.'"

The Right Cat for You: Pedigree or Not?

Perhaps you've dreamed of owning a purebred cat with "star quality"—one that looks beautiful, has the temperament most pleasing to you, and may even lead you into the fascinating world of breeding and showing. On the other hand, a pet-quality purebred may be just what you want to curl up with by the fireplace on a winter night. The untrained eye is unlikely to notice some small attribute that does not meet the exacting standards for show quality, and you and your beautiful kitten can be happy homebodies.

Perhaps Chapter 1 has given you some idea of the cat that will be your soul mate. The five most popular breeds in the United States at this writing are the calm, sweet-tempered Persian; the hale and hearty Maine Coon; the elegant, superbright Siamese; the quiet, Persian-like Exotic Shorthair; and the energetic, affectionate Abyssinian. And that's only the beginning.

One way to narrow down your choices is to talk with breeders and attend local cat shows. You may also have a friend who has a pedigreed cat you admire and who will fill you in on its needs and personality. A wealth of resources for the cat fancier is available in the form of books, magazines, websites, newsletters, pet-supply houses, and other sources, many of which are listed at the end of this book.

In deciding whether your new pet should be a male or a female, it makes little difference unless you plan to breed your pedigreed cat at a future date (which might better be left to the professionals). Otherwise, spaying and neutering at the appropriate time will save you and your cat(s) a great deal of trouble, since unspayed

🐾 *The handsome felines on this page are all purebreds. At left is a bicolor Persian, with its distinctively foreshortened muzzle; at top is an Asian ticked tabby; and, above, a blue Burmese.*

females in heat are both noisy and very troublesome, and unneutered males will mark their territory (your house!) with a very offensive-smelling urine. Male cats are usually somewhat larger than females. They may be a bit more independent, but in general they make equally affectionate and intelligent companions.

Take your time, whether you are choosing a relatively expensive purebred or a healthy cat or kitten that can be adopted from a local shelter or humane association.

Many mixed-breed cats, as mentioned before, are just as appealing and affectionate

as their pedigreed counterparts, and the fact that a larger gene pool is involved in their backgrounds often makes for sturdy constitutions and sound temperament. Without your intervention, these cats might not find the loving home that should be the birthright of every companion animal.

Whether they are purebred or not, all kittens are adorable. And who's to say that these fine cats and kittens are any less appealing than their pedigreed counterparts, shown on the opposite page?

3

Preparations
and Cat Kit

Getting It Together

🐾 *Ideally, you should select a veterinarian on the basis of a personal recommendation, preferably that of another cat owner in your neighborhood.*

Many authorities suggest that the first "item" in your cat kit should be a veterinarian that you choose even before you acquire a cat or kitten. For one thing, you want to be sure of finding a vet in whom you have confidence, and with whom you feel comfortable, since you'll probably be seeing him or her regularly for years to come. Personally, I prefer a vet who is close to home, in case of emergency, and to reduce stress on your pet/s. Most cats hate riding in the car boxed up in a carrier and often vocalize, plaintively or loudly, all the way to the doctor's office. This, in turn, stresses me, which is not especially useful.

Another good reason to preselect a vet is that he or she can be helpful in directing you to reputable breeders, cats whose owners have to give them up, or well-run shelters, where you are most likely to find a kitten or cat in good health—a paramount concern. At the same time, you can inquire about fees and services and ensure that the facility is clean, up-to-date, and staffed by helpful, caring people.

The following checklist will help you determine signs of good health and temperament for yourself, and your prospective pet can be checked by your veterinarian before you bring her home. This will prevent a lot of heartache if he detects a problem and will avoid spreading disease if you already have other pets.

Signs of a Healthy Kitten

- ✔ The eyes should be clear and bright, with no sign of discharge.

- ✔ Look into the ears, which should be clean, with no sign of infection or ear mites (which resemble specks of black dirt).

- ✔ Check that the cat's tongue and gums are pink, not pale.

- ✔ Be sure that the cat is not sneezing and that there is no discharge from the nose.

- ✔ The coat should be clean and shiny, with no bald patches that might indicate mange or some other disorder.

- ✔ Fluff up the fur to see that the skin is free of sores or signs of irritation.

- ✔ Be sure that the abdomen is not distended—a possible indication of internal parasites.

- ✔ If you're adopting a kitten, it should never be less than eight weeks old.

- ✔ The cat's reaction to your gentle handling tells you a good deal about its personality. Does it shy away and try to hide, or does it seem playful, outgoing, and friendly?

First Encounter: Pet and Vet

When you bring your prized choice to the vet, take along with you any health or vaccination records from the breeder or shelter where you adopted her. The initial examination will determine (hopefully) that she is, indeed, in good health. If she was not vaccinated between the ages of six and eight weeks, this should be done now, to protect her against such diseases as feline rhinotracheitis, calicivirus, and

feline distemper. These are generally administered as a single injection. The second set of vaccinations is usually given at twelve weeks and the third at sixteen weeks. Schedules for the cat's annual or intermittent booster shots may vary.

Paws for Thought

🐾 Cats: An Owner's Guide is not designed to supplant professional diagnosis and treatment of feline conditions and disorders. Information given here may sometimes conflict with regional practices and recommendations. Let your veterinarian be your guide.

🐾 State and municipal law varies in the requirements for feline immunization. Some areas now mandate a rabies vaccination, since this deadly disease has spread in recent years. Even if it is not required by your state, you should discuss the possibility of having your cat vaccinated against rabies, especially if she will be allowed outdoors.

🐾 Immunization against feline leukemia is still a matter of debate among some veterinarians. It requires a blood test before administration, since a cat that is already infected by it cannot be helped and may spread the disease to other felines. This vaccine, when given, consists of three injections several weeks apart, followed by an annual booster.

🐾 Note that the American Association of Feline Practitioners (AAFP) recommends that all kittens be vaccinated for rabies, feline panleukopenia, feline viral rhinotracheitis, and feline calicivirus. Vaccines for less common illnesses, including feline leukemia virus, are recommended by the AAFP only for cats at risk. Your vet is your best guide in these matters, and your cat's medical record may be entered on page 251. See later chapters for additional information on pet health care.

The House Beautiful—Feline Style

Before your furry bundle of joy actually comes home, you'll want to acquire the basic supplies she'll need and to ensure that no dangers to her are lurking in the environment.

First, the basics:

- food and water bowls
- scratching post (the taller the better, so long as it's broad-based and won't tip over easily)
- good-quality brush and comb
- litter tray and scoop
  - a sturdy cat carrier
    - a cat bed and/or basket

Most of these items are available in various forms and price ranges, as explained below.

Scratching posts These are available in several surfaces and designs, including carpet, sisal rope, and cardboard. Most are freestanding; some have a handle for hanging from a doorknob. You can make a scratching post yourself by covering a suitable material, like a plywood slantboard

"Confounding my human,
I ask out, having entered;
ask in, having outed,
and nip the naked heel.
Reason me no reasons.
I go by other stars."

—Peter Neumeyer

times a day. If you have a large, screened porch, you may wish to place a cat flap in the window of an adjacent room so Kitty can enjoy the sun and air. These flaps are quite simple to install and may be obtained in both the standard and lockable forms.

or column, with the material your cat seems to prefer. Or use vertical and horizontal crossbars of untreated wood. Space and finances permitting, you may wish to try the "kitty condo" approach mentioned on page 153—multilevel climbing perches that may double as beds.

Cat flaps These can be inserted into windows and doors to allow your pet access to protected areas without opening and closing the door a dozen

If you have a two-story dwelling, it's a good idea to have a litter box on each level, especially when your cat is aging or not in robust health. This will make life easier for both of you, since a well-trained cat does not want to soil the house, nor do you need the mess. If an accident does occur, have a bottle of enzyme carpet cleaner with a built-in odor neutralizer on hand to clean up the stain and the smell. Otherwise, your kitten or cat may continue to void or eliminate on that spot.

Feeding equipment Many pet owners prefer having utensils—knife, fork, spoon, can opener—reserved for the use of their cat or dog. Basic ceramic bowls for food and water are inexpensive and can be cleaned at high temperatures that kill bacteria. Stainless steel bowls are also serviceable, as are wide-based plastic bowls. A double food-and-water bowl has the advantage of being tip-proof, but the cat often deposits bits of food in his water dish after eating—or maybe just to make more work for you.

Types of litter With the ever-growing interest in pet cats, litter types have proliferated in recent years. They range from the inexpensive, traditional clay type to scoopable, clumping clay that is flushable and more odor-absorbent, crystals of silica sand, and pellets made of recycled newspapers, grass fiber, or wood pulp. A plastic litter scoop can be found at the supermarket for cleaning the box at least once a day.

If you have two boxes, you may try several types of litter to see which your new kitten or cat seems to prefer. The traditional clay type is the least expensive, but it tends to track onto your floors and is quite dusty. The paper- and plant-fiber types have the advantage of being trackless and dust-free. They can also be recycled as mulch or compost. If you decide to switch from one litter to another, introduce the new one a little at a time by combining it with the old one until your pet grows accustomed to it.

If desired, you can purchase an electronic-timer food dispenser for about forty dollars. This is worthwhile if you sometimes spend the night away from home and may also prevent the chubby cat from eating two days' rations at a single sitting! Self-regulating water bowls ensure an adequate supply of fresh drinking water at all times.

Litter boxes A new kitten will need an accessible plastic litter box no more than two inches high, preferably placed in a low-traffic area and away from food and water bowls. A deeper box, or one with a hood, can be purchased for the full-grown pet. Be sure that it is sufficiently large to accommodate him. Male Maine Coons, for example, may tip the scale at more than twenty pounds. Some owners prefer the relatively expensive convenience of the self-cleaning litter box, which rakes through the litter after the cat has stepped out and drops the waste into a receptacle below for easy disposal.

Your kitten will soon learn to use the litter tray consistently, especially if you keep a good eye on him during the early days while he's in training.

Bed and bedding There are many comfortable types of cat beds available through your local pet-supply stores or from reputable mail-order companies and websites.

They come in every conceivable color and design, from the cozy, plush-covered "cuddler" and "cave" types to opulent pillows and orthopedic beds. Waterproof and heated pads can raise your kitty's comfort level, and some pets like to bed down or play for hours in cat tunnels or sacks embellished with pom-poms or other soft toys.

For the multicat household, there are, as you would imagine, multibeds and even basket bunk beds!

Cats will always seek out the most comfortable spots in the house, regardless of whether that means getting cozy on your new cream sofa (right) or sprawling out on top of—or even inside!—your laundry basket (above). To make life easier for yourself, invest in an irresistible cat bed.

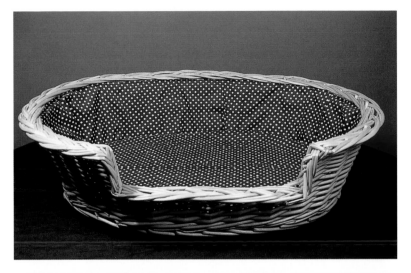

😺 *The traditional cat basket remains a popular choice of bed, but remember that a removable, washable lining or separate bedding should be used inside the basket. Washable fake-fur pads, blankets, or throws positioned in a draft-free, cozy corner will soon attract your cat, too.*

Wearability and washability of the covering should be prime considerations. Your cat may scratch or pluck at the bedding or bring in fleas or other creatures from outdoors, so make sure that you concentrate on practicality. Of course, none of these attractions will prevent your cat from sleeping on your bed, but cats are privacy-loving animals and enjoy having a spot of their own for luxurious snoozes, even if it's a cardboard box.

Feline Facts

😺 Cats catch colds easily, and older animals are susceptible to rheumatism and arthritis, just as we are. Their beds should never be placed in a drafty area or in a cold, damp basement.

Tooth Trouble

- ✓ Bad breath
- ✓ Inflamed gums
- ✓ Plaque and tartar buildup
- ✓ Discomfort when eating dry food
- ✓ Drooling
- ✓ Depressed appetite
- ✓ Enlarged lymph nodes in the neck

If your cat is long-haired, you already know that she will need daily grooming with a brush and comb to prevent mats from forming and reduce the incidence of hair balls. A soft natural-bristle brush and a wide-toothed comb are recommended. You may also use talcum powder to fluff up her beautiful coat and reduce any oiliness. Most longhairs benefit from periodic baths, which, again, are best introduced at an early age. You'll need an ample,

🐾 *Use a rubber mitt (below, left) to groom short-haired cats and a combination of wire slicker brushes (top) and wide-toothed combs (below) or rake combs (opposite) to prevent matting and hair balls in your long-haired cat. Soft natural-bristle brushes are also recommended for long, fluffy coats.*

Groomed to Purrfection

Grooming basics include nail clippers, comb, brush, toothbrush, and veterinary toothpaste, as well as cotton balls for cleaning the face and wiping any harmless discharge from the eyes—Persians are especially prone to this problem and may need to have the corners of their eyes wiped daily. Your vet can show you how to brush your cat's teeth at home, ideally starting at an early age to prevent dental disease and eventual tooth loss. Gauze pads and cotton swabs can also be used to remove plaque and help keep tartar from forming. Watch for the signs of dental disease (see the following checklist) in your adult cat, any of which mandate a trip to the veterinarian.

escape-proof basin, a pet shampoo, a soft cloth for washing, a plastic pitcher for rinsing, and a towel to dry her off before you continue with her grooming routine. Additional tips on bathing your pet can be obtained from your vet's office, an experienced breeder, a groomer, or one of the many excellent magazines that cater to cats.

🐾 *A short coat should be brushed regularly or groomed with a mitt or chamois leather.*

Your short-haired cat or kitten will benefit by regular brushing with a bristle or rubber brush, as well as combing, to remove dead hair from the coat and bring natural oils and gloss to the surface by the gentle massaging action. Chamois leather enhances the appearance of the coat as well, and your pet will enjoy the soft stroking involved.

🐾 *A Birman's coat is long and silky and should be groomed daily with a brush and comb.*

Paws for Thought

🐾 Combine a kitten's first grooming sessions with plenty of play to accustom him to the brushes, mitts, and other equipment, and keep the early sessions brief.

🐾 If you are a first-time owner, a demonstration of grooming techniques from a vet or groomer is recommended in preference to following written guidelines, especially if your pet is skittish.

🐾 Acquiring an array of grooming tools is only a first step to an effective grooming routine; using these tools correctly and regularly requires commitment and time.

🐾 A thorough grooming routine will help you to keep an eye on your cat's health and well-being, enabling you to identify skin and coat problems, the presence of ticks and other mites, and the condition of the teeth, ears, claws, and eyes.

Come Out and Play!

One of the most rewarding and amusing ways of bonding with your kitten or cat is through play. You may feel like a child in a candy store when you go shopping for Kitty's new toys.

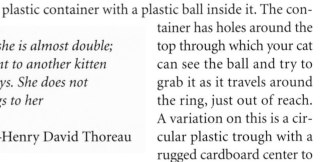

Attractive playthings can be found at pet-supply stores to entice your cat, ranging from stuffed mice to furry balls, jingle-bell and cage balls, battery-operated

Endless amusement is derived from watching your adorable kitten entertain herself with a favorite toy.

ground or bounce it along the floor, and your pet will go into stalking mode, then pounce on the feather—unless you lift it away. When he leaps into the air to capture it, you can redirect it to another spot to keep the game going as long as you like.

toys that project an elusive laser beam across the floor for chasing, and countless catnip-refillable toys in the shape of birds, dinosaurs, elephants, and even—sweet revenge—dogs.

"Tease toys" are another best-seller. They resemble a short fishing rod attached to a length of strong cord to which a feather is secured. This is an interactive toy that most cats love. You may dangle the feather a few inches from the

"A kitten is so flexible that she is almost double; the hind parts are equivalent to another kitten with which the forepart plays. She does not discover that her tail belongs to her until you tread on it."

—Henry David Thoreau

Another amusing activity is the ball-trap toy, a round plastic container with a plastic ball inside it. The container has holes around the top through which your cat can see the ball and try to grab it as it travels around the ring, just out of reach. A variation on this is a circular plastic trough with a rugged cardboard center to be used as a scratching pad. Here, the plastic ball rolls around the trough in plain view and can be readily batted out again and again.

Cats are also intrigued by toys you can provide without spending any money at all. A ball of wadded-up paper is a favorite with cats who like to play fetch or prefer to simply bat it around the room. (Make sure that you do not offer balls made of plastic wrap or aluminum foil, both of which are dangerous.)

Ribbons, yarn, string, or stuffed toys outgrown by children can be dangled from a sturdy piece of elastic taped in a doorway. These will attract immediate attention, with the added advantage that your pet won't be able to ingest them since they can't be detached.

A sunny windowsill, perhaps padded with carpeting or pillows, is an agreeable vantage point from which to watch birds, pets, and people outside.

You can also construct "cat towns" from cardboard cartons turned upside down and arranged to make tunnels and secret hideouts with doorways cut here and there.

Even an outdoor cat run is affordable, if you can improvise a strong enclosure from boards and screening, with shelves at various heights. This is also the safest way to let your pet enjoy the outdoors, free from the threat of stray dogs, traffic, pesticides, and other hazards.

Paws for Thought

🐾 Be sure no toy is small enough to be swallowed by your cat.

🐾 Pick up toys after play so family members don't trip and injure themselves.

🐾 Rotate favorite toys so your cat doesn't get bored with them.

🐾 Add fresh catnip to refillable toys as needed so they remain alluring.

🐾 *Bells are useful to alert birds to the presence of your cat—and to help you find her if she's hiding from you.*

Tags imprinted with your cat's name and your address and phone number are readily ordered through your vet's office, pet stores, or mail-order catalog. They come in the form of disks, bones, hearts, and other whimsical shapes, as you prefer. If you plan to leash-train your cat, this is best begun indoors, and a harness is recommended over a collar for safety's sake. A kitten will probably become accustomed (gradually) to a harness and leash more readily than a mature cat, which, if it lets you put the harness on at all, may lie down and flatly refuse to move. Patience is the keyword here. Some breeds, like the Himalayan, seem to bask in the attention they receive on outings in their brightly colored accoutrements.

🐾 *Breakaway, or release-type, buckles come undone when tugged sharply, for your cat's safety. This type of collar is not suitable, however, for use with a leash.*

Whose Kitty Are You?

Even if you plan to keep your pet entirely indoors, he must have a collar and identification tags in case he goes astray. There are any number of decorative collars available, from tartans and solid colors to zebra stripes and wildcat patterns. You may also need the more utilitarian flea collar to prevent pesky critters brought in from outside from taking up residence on your cat or kitten. Any type of collar used for a cat should be of the breakaway type—that is, if it catches on something, it will snap off to prevent accidental strangulation on a tree limb or under a fence. Belled collars are a good way to help protect the local bird life.

🐾 *Collars should be durable, washable, comfortable, and carefully fitted. Nylon is the most popular material today, but leather collars are also available.*

Never transport a cat without a purpose-designed carrier. You can choose among a wide variety of sturdy materials, including wire, cardboard (the least expensive), plastic, and wicker. In all cases, the carrier should be large enough for the cat or kitten to turn around in comfortably and, of course, well ventilated. For longer trips, you will need food and water cups that attach to the grated end of the carrier. If you plan to travel by air, you will need to invest in a hard-sided, airline-approved carrier that will be labeled "Live Animal/s" in a fluorescent color. Your kitty may grumble a bit, but he is assured of a happy landing and your mind will be at ease about his welfare in transit.

Persuading a reluctant cat to cooperate when you attempt to put him in a carrier can be very challenging! Make sure that you accustom your new kitten to his carrier by tempting him to play in it before you need to transport him anywhere.

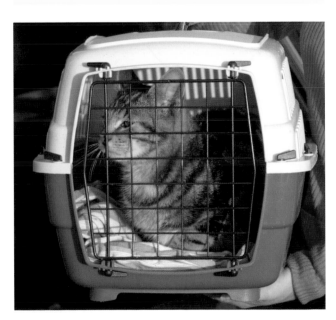

4

Bringing Kitty Home

Now that you've prepared all the essentials for making your new cat or kitten welcome, it's time to bring your pet home and help her settle in at a relaxed pace. This is an exciting time, but restrain your enthusiasm so as not to overstress the cat, which will almost certainly be uneasy in a strange environment. It would be wise to select a quiet room in which the new arrival can become acclimated for a few days with all its necessities close at hand—food, water, bed, and litter box.

You might add a piece of bedding from the animal's former home to the bed you have prepared for it, especially in the case of a kitten, who will be reassured by the scent of its mother and littermates. If certain rooms and potentially hazardous sites, like the area under the sink where you keep cleaning

🐾 *Whether a tiny kitten or a mature cat, no feline enjoys the experience of moving to a new environment. Your new cat may seek out a hiding place and refuse to be tempted out for several days—even if you've provided a much cozier place for her.*

supplies, are to be off-limits, set these boundaries at once as the cat begins to explore more freely. A firm "no" repeated several times early on can help reduce long-term disputes about forbidden territory. This includes climbing draperies and scratching the sofa and other furniture.

If your cat is to live entirely indoors, even if you have your own house and garden rather than an apartment, it is not wise to let him venture outside at any time. Your pet will inevitably be intrigued by the outdoors and will soon try to escape from the house at

🐾 *Despite your thoughtful planning in setting up a safe, fun, and comfortable space in your home for Kitty, she's bound to prefer your computer desk or hazard-filled kitchen cabinets. Keep these places firmly closed off.*

control methods with your veterinarian before you allow your cat to eat any outdoor plants. This also applies to indoor plants treated for spider mites and other troublesome creatures with pesticides.)

every opportunity. Statistics indicate that indoor cats live longer since they are at far less risk of acquiring diseases and fleas or other parasites, or of incurring injuries caused by fighting, not to mention the dangers posed by automobiles and other traffic hazards.

However, if your garden is safely fenced or you can tether your cat nearby while you garden, the experience will be enriching for both of you. Organic gardening will ensure that your pet will not be exposed to harmful herbicides or pesticides, and that he can safely enjoy eating plants like lemongrass and thyme, which repel fleas and other insects. (Warning: Be sure to check your garden pest-

Paws for Thought

🐾 When a new kitten is brought home, many owners have found it helpful to put a wind-up clock (no alarms, please!) under the kitten's bedding, or nearby, so it is reassured by the ticking sound, which resembles that of a heartbeat.

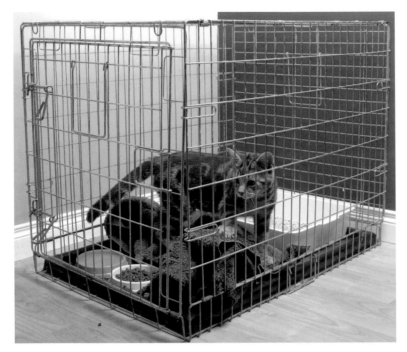

How to Make a Neglected or Mistreated Cat Comfortable in Your Home

If you have been so kind as to adopt a cat that has suffered from neglect or outright maltreatment, it will take much time and patient care to bond with it, but the results will far outweigh the effort. The key here is "easy does it." The cat must not be forced into stressful situations that recall the original trauma; on the contrary, its boundaries must be respected. A quiet, soothing tone of voice is essential, and rewards in the form of food treats or a meal will help immeasurably in establishing trust and confidence.

Many people do not realize that the most sensitive period for socializing a kitten occurs during its first four to seven weeks. At this time, the young animal develops attachments to people and to other animals most easily. In fact, if the kitten has had no human contact before it reaches twelve weeks of age, its future ability to live comfortably with people and members of its own and other species is seriously compromised. Add to this the trauma experienced by a young or full-grown cat that has been actively mistreated in its former environment and you have a very challenging situation. However, there are many commonsense solutions that will help both you and the cat to become comfortable in a safe, nurturing environment.

One method is to keep the newcomer in a large wire cage that can accommodate a litter box at one end, food and water at the other, and a bed in between. When first acclimating the cat or kitten to the environment, the cage should be placed in a very quiet room, perhaps with a cloth draped over part of it, or a three-sided box inside that offers a sense of security. Only the caretaker should feed, water, and clean the litter box at this early stage.

As the animal begins to relax and show some interest in its surroundings, the cage can be moved to rooms where there is more household activity. Since spitting and hissing are the animal's instinctive responses to situations perceived as threatening, do not be surprised if this defensive behavior and body language continues for some time. Children, guests, and other pets must not be allowed near the newcomer until he becomes less sensitive and more curious, which may well take some time, especially if the cat has never lived indoors before.

😺 *The sadly neglected kitten at right is a distressing sight, but its injuries are relatively superficial. With the benefit of a loving home it should soon look as pampered and privileged as the successfully rescued cat above.*

Nicholas Dodman, D.V.M., in his book *The Cat Who Cried for Help,* describes the process by which he and his wife won over a deeply mistrustful and frightened cat named Cinder: "Basically, she never came out from under the furniture and was rarely seen unless she was scurrying from one hiding place to another. . . . Some days we could tell we had cats only by the fact that the food we put down disappeared and from the telltale signs in the litter box."

The Dodmans dealt with the problem by spending every evening in the room where Cinder hid, sitting quietly on the sofa, reading, and occasionally tossing her a food treat. To make the treat more attractive, they took up her food dish late in the afternoon. Over a period of months,

she became bolder about retrieving the treats, until finally, she was taking food from their hands and even sitting on their laps to be petted. Even so, she still became terrified when visitors came into the house. Dr. Dodman notes that: "The cure for this was along similar lines: gradual exposure and pleasant consequences. We never forced her to meet anyone she didn't want to and simply allowed her to make friends at her own pace, rewarding every step of the way."

🐾 *If your cat has taken up residence on the top of the china cabinet because she's anxious, don't reach up to retrieve her forcibly. You'll only make her more nervous—and she might express her fear through her claws! Instead, find an irresistibly tempting treat to encourage her back down, or simply leave her be until she's ready to rejoin the household at floor level*

Other Ways of Reducing Your Pet's Anxiety

Sometimes cat owners inadvertently contribute to fearful behaviors by trying to calm the cat when it is anxious. This generally

results in actually reinforcing the anxious response. Never carry a nervous pet toward a visitor or other fear-producing stimulus. The cat will feel trapped and may injure its handler in its attempt to get away. In recent years, veterinary medicine, humane associations, and professionals skilled at working with cats

accompany acute anxiety, including increased heart rate, respiration, and blood distribution, subside. But when the animal can't recognize the source of its fear, such as random loud noises outside by construction workers or passing vehicles, it can develop anxiety disorders comparable to those in humans.

Any cat that develops these symptoms should be taken to your regular veterinarian for a complete checkup. Medical causes for the anxious behav-

have discovered many factors that contribute to stress in cats and the means of reducing it. Stress is a critical factor in most behavior problems. It may be expressed in a variety of ways, including inappropriate elimination, destructive scratching, overgrooming, excessive vocalization, biting, and other undesirable activities. Like most other mammals, cats that feel threatened have four major defense strategies: flight, fight, freeze, and appeasement. Unlike dogs, cats—especially female cats with kittens—rarely choose appeasement, but will stand and fight even a larger foe. Where the stress response can be resolved by a simple choice—say, flight—the cat soon returns to its original, relaxed state. The physiological changes that

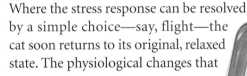

ior should be evaluated before the problem is assumed to be behavioral. If it is, a number of medications may be prescribed over the short term. More permanent solutions may include covering a window from which your cat regularly sees an animal outside (territorial invasion), offering him more opportunities for active play, rethinking changes in daily routine that may have distressed him, relieving overcrowding of the house, and helping him cope with the loss of a fellow pet. In such cases, you can ask your veterinarian to refer you to a professional who is experienced in working with cats.

What to Do if Your Pet Is Hiding

What *not* to do is quite obvious: Dragging the frightened animal from its refuge is not a good idea, except in cases of extreme danger, such as a fire. Hiding or freezing to avoid notice is quite common among cats who have recently been introduced to the household, whether a one-person apartment or a larger, noisier venue. They often disappear under beds, hide behind draperies, or find an inaccessible spot behind the sofa in which to acclimate themselves.

Once they have been introduced to the litter box and the place where their food and water bowls are to be stationed, they should be allowed to take their time in exploring their new environment and owner(s). It often takes some weeks, especially with an adult cat, for a sense of familiarity to develop. Make sure you are unobtrusive but available as they begin to overcome their shyness and make longer forays into new rooms and areas that are not blocked off for their safety or to protect your valuables.

Paws for Thought

🐾 Virtually all cats will go into hiding if a move is impending. The disarray of the house, the owner's excitement or anxiety, and the intrusion of strange people in droves are enough to send the best-balanced cat into a tizzy. Be sure your pet is confined to a single, locked room during these operations, with their food, water, bedding, litter box, and carrier close at hand for last-minute packing and transport. Similarly, do not let your cat escape from the new house. Only 3 percent of cats who are lost or have strayed are eventually reunited with their owners through a shelter or animal-control facility.

Kittens, with their insatiable curiosity, are usually less reticent than mature cats about exploring a new environment, especially if you have acquired a pair that are littermates. They will be friends for life and reinforce each other's sense of safety wherever they are.

Whether pedigree or nonpedigree, if your space and budget permit, it is a good idea to bring home two kittens, especially if you are away from home much of the day. Then your concern is more likely to be cat-proofing the house or a room, rather than hunting them down in closets and draperies. They are much likelier to adapt themselves happily to a new environment, providing they have not been weaned too soon. Eight weeks is the minimum before they leave their mothers.

🐾 *The tabby kitten shown above is already allowing his curiosity to get the better of his fears of the new environment. He'll be out exploring in no time. At left, a mature cat takes a little longer to acclimate to her new surroundings. Eventually, she'll venture out to look for her food bowl or litter box.*

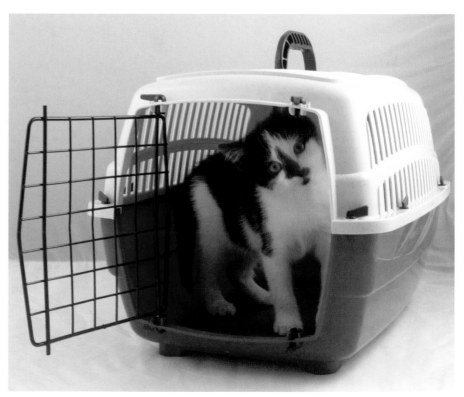

Providing Cozy Corners for Your Pet

In today's marketplace, there is virtually no end to the products that are available to make your pet feel comfortable and secure. We all like our privacy, and cats share this human trait to a much higher degree than dogs, which are essentially pack animals that have been domesticated to make their owners the "leader of the pack."

As you probably know from experience, many cats have a limited tolerance for being petted or picked up and held, especially as one would hold a baby, which translates to "upside down" in feline language. They may even bite or scratch when they have had enough interaction and are ready to go their own ways for a while. The following signals will alert you to the fact that your cat is ready to take a time-out from petting: restlessness, twitching the tail, holding the ears back, attempting to bite you, and extending the claws in readiness for scratching.

If you have provided cozy corners for your pet, she will seek them out when she has had enough interaction with people or other animals in the household. Such corners may include a padded basket, a comfortably lined attachment to the windowsill, a covered hideaway entered by a small opening, or a seat on one of the many cat trees that are available now. These are especially good for a multicat household with limited space, since their verticality provides several perches at once.

Time-honored hiding spaces under the bed, in the closet, or behind the draperies will be discovered by your pet without any help from you. The litter box area should be

🐾 *Your cat's preferred hangout may be her basket or carrier, but she might otherwise discover one herself.*

Some of the perches are accessed by jumping from one level to another, which also provides valuable exercise; others are entered from an opening inside the base. The resting places are padded, fabric-covered shapes that include baskets, tunnels, half-rounds, shelves, and more.

screened for reasons of both privacy and hygiene, and be sure, in catproofing your home, that there are no areas behind bookcases and other furniture in which your cat could get stuck.

So-called "kitty condos" may include still other features: built-in scratching posts, gyms, padded steps for older animals—even a carpet-covered birdhouse at the top!

All these features provide serious comfort for your pet while saving wear and tear—and hair—on your furniture.

Obviously, there are other options available at less expense that you can use as well. A cardboard box with a hole in it, turned upside down, is a ready refuge.

Introducing Your Pet to Children

Most children are irresistibly attracted to pets, and will form mutually beneficial relationships with them, providing they are old enough to learn respect and careful handling. From the start, the child should be taught how to hold the cat properly, providing support under the chest and the hind legs. The sensitive stomach area should not be touched, as the cat or kitten will react with its "grab and bite" reflex.

It is essential to teach the child some of the basics of feline body language, for his own safety. He should be aware that he needs to back off when he sees the ears flatten, the tail twitch, and the hairs along the cat's spine and tail "fluff up." Of course, he should be

🐾 A small child doesn't understand how threatening her behavior may seem from a cat's point of view, and, below the age of six or so, may be too young to learn how to repect its boundaries. Older children, though, will soon earn a kitten's trust—and will derive enormous pleasure from doing so.

"Time spent with cats is never wasted."
—Colette

😺 *Teach your child how to hold the cat comfortably, supporting his hindquarters. Even a reluctant cat will probably "break down" and accept a youngster's enthusiastic attentions if he's not handled too roughly or taken by surprise. Don't leave cats or kittens and young children together without supervision, though.*

warned never to touch a stray cat or a neighbor's pet that he does not know, as serious consequences could follow. These warnings are not designed to create fear in the child, but to raise his awareness of boundaries and protect his safety.

In an article entitled "Feline Care," the organization Cats International advises that: "If you have children under six or seven years of age, it is best not to adopt a kitten under four months old. An overly affectionate toddler can injure a small kitten with a well-meaning hug. A more mature kitten or cat can better withstand a young child's noise and quick movements, but even an adult cat may swat at a tail-pulling child. The key to harmonious interactions between young children and cats is *adult* supervision." This maxim applies to visiting children as well as one's own.

A loving relationship between children and cats can be thwarted by well-meaning parents who try to teach responsibility by putting a child (or children) who is not ready for the responsi-

bility in charge of the pet's care. The child is likely to be forgetful or distracted, leaving the food and water bowls unfilled and the litter box dirty. It is the cat who will suffer from this kind of neglect.

It is probably wiser to delegate other simple household chores to children and have an adult take care of the pet. The good example set by conscientious care is worth far more than the nagging and scolding that may actually create resentment toward the animal on the part of the children. Far better to let all concerned enjoy the relationship with the cat on the cat's own terms, without jeopardizing its well-being.

For a kitten and a young child, establishing a relationship is a learning curve. Spike is a mellow kitten who's been well socialized from the beginning, and he's learned to keep a watchful eye on Jade while they're together. Jade has been taught not to approach Spike suddenly or surprise him. Here, they are shown getting to know each other a little better while playing house.

🐾 *Spike's had enough of the game now, and Jade is leaving him to take a nap in peace.*

How to Handle Your New Cat or Kitten

Common sense and some simple guidelines will help you in handling both kittens and adult cats that are new to your home.

First, the kitten. As he is becoming acclimated, pick him up gently at least once a day and speak to him soothingly in a quiet voice. Hold him for five minutes or so before setting him down in a favorite spot.

After a few days, sit down while holding him and pet him gently while speaking to him. Do not encourage rough play like scratching or biting. If he tries to do this, tell him "no" firmly and put him down. (It's a myth that cats can't be taught the difference between acceptable and unacceptable behaviors.)

Never try to pick him up by the scruff of his neck, as a mother cat does. You're not a cat and could possibly injure him. Safe handling involves placing one hand around his stomach and the other under his hind legs. Support his head and neck gently.

As he grows accustomed to being handled and enjoys it, you can stroll around the room quietly while holding and talking to him. Shortly thereafter, begin to place him on a well-lighted table and familiarize him with the kind of handling that will be involved in routine health checks and grooming.

Pick up a paw and press gently to extend the claws. Next time, look into his ears to check for wax, dirt, and ear mites. Later, you can open his mouth and extend your finger along the gum line. It will be easy to clean his teeth, clip his toenails, and perform other grooming tasks once he is comfortable with these routines, and the bonding process will be enhanced at the same time.

Depending upon its previous owners, the adult cat new to your household will present more of a challenge when it comes to handling. As mentioned earlier in this chapter, you want to give the newcomer plenty of leeway as he makes the gradual transition to a new owner and environment. Your cat will let you know when he is ready to be petted or picked up, and it's most unlikely that this will happen before some weeks have elapsed, or even longer. From these beginnings, you can follow the general guidelines above in getting your cat accustomed to regular health checkups at home and to the regular grooming and caretaking that both of you will enjoy during the weeks, months, and years to come.

Let Go of Your Cat When He Displays these Signals:

- ✔ Becoming restless
- ✔ Twitching his tail
- ✔ Turning his ears back or flicking them back and forth
- ✔ Moving his head toward your hand
- ✔ Seizing your wrist with his forepaws, claws unsheathed

🐾 *An adult cat that hasn't been handled sensitively from a young age will probably take some time to submit to your attentions. Treat him with patience, but don't give up when he resists, because the day will come when you'll need to pick him up and put him in his carrier. Keep the sessions brief and calm.*

Introducing Your Cat to Other Pets

In *Cats and Kittens* magazine (November 2002), Phil Maggitti offers humorous and sensible advice on introducing a new kitten to the resident cat in your household. As he points out:

"Unfortunately, most cat owners who decide to add another cat to their cabals do not stop to consider the gravity of their ambitions. They assume that all they have to do is call a meeting, take the new cat out of its carrier, present it to the old cat and say, 'Stonewall, this is General Grant. He's going to be playing with your toys, using your litter pan, drinking from your water bowl and sharing the bed with us. Isn't he cute?'"

Naturally, those who have read this book thus far would never make such a mistake! As discussed previously, a major consid-

Animals are such agreeable friends; they ask no questions; they pass no criticisms.
—George Eliot

eration before acquiring a new kitten or cat is the number and kind of pet(s) already in your household. A pet rabbit in a pen will pose little or no problem should you decide to bring home a new kitten or cat, but another cat or a dog will require some careful introductions.

A period of "quarantine" in a separate room for several days is recommended for the newcomer, so he can take the measure of his surroundings before meeting the cat already in residence. Then he should be placed in his carrier and the door opened so that "Stonewall" can conduct a short pre-screening interview. Repeat this for several weeks, until

both parties are ready for unfettered, but not unsupervised, contact. If these encounters are successful for three or four days in a row, you can feel confident that the potential combatants are getting acquainted, but do not leave them alone in the house until you are sure that the truce they've established has become a peace.

Some suggestions for introducing Fido to the newcomer are listed on pages 122–3. A dog who has grown up with cats will usually give the new arrival an enthusiastic, if not boisterous, welcome, but be sure that the cat has time to get used to the dog's presence before there is any—again, supervised—contact between them.

Proper dog training is essential in these introductions: "Sit" and "stay" must be obeyed at once to prevent the dog from chasing or otherwise attempting to play with the cat before it feels safe. Once the cat is confident that the dog does not pose a threat, it is very likely that a close friendship will develop between them.

🐾 *Kittens will learn to accept each other fairly quickly, but it's a much better idea to adopt two littermates to avoid the introduction process (opposite). Fred, shown at right, reacted with alarming enthusiasm when Snowball moved in, but now he's learned to respect her—and, of course, she's taught him who's boss.*

5
Why Does Kitty
Do That?

The following time line will give you an idea of what to expect from your cat during the various developmental stages from birth through kittenhood, maturity, breeding (unless spayed or neutered), mothering, and old age. The rest of the chapter explains feline habits and behavior across a broad spectrum and helps you understand your cat's body language and voice in all their ramifications.

You may be surprised at the many nuances expressed by the cat's meow, which appears to be reserved for conversations with humans. And when cats communicate with each other, there are almost a hundred different sounds and tones that they can use, including the hair-raising screeches and guttural growls of a full-fledged cat fight!

Birth and Early Life

🐾 Most kittens weigh about three and a half ounces at birth.

🐾 They are born blind and deaf, but sense their mother's bodily warmth and strive to stay close to her.

🐾 They need to receive their mother's colostrum, or "first milk," within forty-eight hours to benefit from the vital antibody protection it provides.

🐾 Many kittens will begin purring at one day old; most show the reflex to right themselves when flipped over.

🐾 At one week, the newborn kittens are usually nursing or sleeping. Sex can be determined by looking underneath the tail. (Female cats have less space between the anal opening and the genitals than male cats.)

🐾 Their weight at one week should have doubled since birth, and the stump of umbilical cord should have fallen off, leaving no sign of infection or inflammation.

Two to Four Weeks:

🐾 At two weeks, the kitten's ears have opened and its eyes are beginning to open, although vision is still unclear.

🐾 The eyes should be blue; final adult eye color will come later.

🐾 Optimum socialization begins at this time, when the kittens should be handled gently and talked to softly each day for brief periods.

🐾 At three weeks, kittens can eliminate without stimulation by the mother cat. They are learning to stand up, though wobbly, and are crawling vigorously. Learning through exploration begins at this time.

🐾 At four weeks of age, the kitten's eyes are completely open and the baby, or milk, teeth start to appear. Balance is developing and littermates begin to enjoy rolling and tumbling with one another.

🐾 The kittens are learning to groom themselves.

Five to Ten Weeks:

🐾 At five weeks, balance continues to improve and all senses are working.

🐾 Kittens will make tentative efforts to eat solid food; their baby teeth are still coming in.

🐾 They may experiment with digging and scratching in the litter box.

🐾 Weaning begins at six weeks and should be complete by nine weeks.

🐾 At seven weeks, the kitten's weight is about seven times that at birth.

😺 The kitten has all its baby teeth at seven weeks.

😺 Littermates engage in mock fighting and hunting, which helps establish dominance patterns and develop strength and agility.

😺 Nonpedigree cats of pet quality may be scheduled for spaying or neutering any time between the ages of six and twelve weeks.

😺 At around eight weeks, the kittens receive their initial vaccinations against the potentially lethal diseases they may be at risk of contracting.

😺 By ten weeks of age, the grace and balance of the adult feline is becoming apparent as the kittens leap, stride, and climb with ever-increasing confidence.

Three to Six Months:

🐾 Adult eye color has appeared and coat patterns are now well defined.

🐾 Adult teeth have replaced baby teeth and the mother cat completes late weaning by denying kittens access to her nipples.

🐾 Personality and temperament are established by the age of four months when the "magic window" of socialization closes (some cat behaviorists believe that it closes even sooner).

🐾 At five months of age, kittens begin scent-marking their territory.

🐾 At six months, signs of sexual maturity appear in females. Pets who were not spayed as juveniles should be scheduled for spay surgery to prevent breeding.

Seven Months to One Year

🐾 Growth continues more slowly and males reach sexual maturity.

🐾 Nonpedigree males should be neutered now if juvenile surgery was not scheduled.

🐾 In long-haired cats, the full adult coat appears.

🐾 Cats have become acclimated to their families, including any other pets, and to household routines.

🐾 Breeding: See pages 208–9 and 226–31 for information on pregnancy.

Maturity

The following table gives a rough idea of how cats age vis-à-vis humans, beginning at the age of one year:

CAT'S AGE	COMPARABLE HUMAN AGE
1 year	15 years
2 years	24 years
4 years	32 years
6 years	40 years
8 years	48 years
10 years	56 years
12 years	64 years
14 years	72 years
16 years	80 years
18 years	88 years
20 years	96 years
21 years	100 years

Your cat may be considered in the prime of his or her life between the ages of one and nine years, although, like us, not all cats age at the same rate. During these years, with appropriate diet, exercise, grooming, and veterinary care, your feline friend should flourish, as evidenced by clear eyes, alert hearing, lustrous coat, agility, activity, good temperament, and other signs of vitality.

A cat's normal temperature varies between 101.5 and 102.5°F (38.6 to 39.2°C). It can be taken with a conventional medical thermometer smeared with a little vegetable oil or petroleum jelly. (**Caution:** Have your vet demonstrate how to do this gently and carefully. There is a high risk of causing internal damage.) If it rises to more than 103.5°F, you should call your veterinarian.

Remember, too, that your cat's emotional well-being is just as important as his physical well-being. A loving, stress-free environment will keep your pet happy and secure well into his golden years.

Mothering

As mentioned earlier, it is *strongly* recommended that pet-quality males and females be neutered and spayed respectively by responsible owners to prevent the birth of kittens that will end up in animal shelters, be destroyed, or left to fend for themselves as feral outcasts.

Several long-standing myths have contributed to the overpopulation of the cat world. One is that having a litter of kittens is healthier for a female. Another is that altered cats become obese.

However, we include this section to provide a comprehensive overview of feline behavior, including the vigilant and courageous care provided by the mother cat. The usual gestation period ranges between sixty-three and sixty-five days, and the pregnant female will seek out a suitable spot for delivery as her time grows near.

It is best to provide a roomy cardboard box or plastic laundry basket lined with absorbent towels, in hopes that she will choose it rather than delivering her kittens in the basement or a dresser drawer! However, if she gives birth in an undesirable spot, she should not be disturbed until all the kittens are born. (Be sure that your vet is aware of your pet's due date in case any help is needed.)

As each kitten is born, the mother will tear open the amniotic sac with her teeth

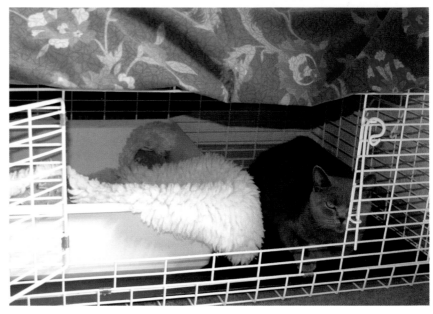

and clean the kitten's nose and mouth of mucus. Then she will lick the newborn to stimulate its respiratory and circulatory systems, and bite off the umbilical cord, which she eats along with the placenta. This provides hormones that help to bring on lactation.

🐾 *Introduce the "queen" to a box or laundry basket lined with soft towels when she's nearly due. She should begin to scratch and "nest" in the basket or box as her due date approaches. Purpose-designed whelping boxes and cages also include a guard rail around the inside walls to prevent the mother accidentally suffocating a newborn, though this misfortune happens only rarely.*

The delivery is complete when all the afterbirths have been expelled, as indicated by a discharge that's dark red or reddish-brown in color. If the mother cat has used the box prepared for her, replace the soiled towels and newspapers with fresh bedding. If she's given birth elsewhere, gently remove the kittens to the box and she will join them at once.

The new family should be left alone to get the kittens accustomed to nursing, each at its own teat, for the first twenty-four hours, when they ingest the essential colostrum, or first milk, mentioned previously. Provide the mother with as much food as she will accept while nursing to ensure adequate milk production and keep a discreet eye on the kittens to make sure that all is well.

It is important to keep the box clean and to check the mother's abdomen daily to make sure her teats are not caked with milk. Keep the "nursery" free of bright lights and disruptive noises, as the mother will move the kittens if she feels they are threatened in any way. Ideally, she will produce an adequate supply of milk until the kittens are ready to be weaned. If the kittens are not gaining weight or appear to be struggling to feed, contact your veterinarian. Kitten mush can be introduced to begin the weaning process at around three to four weeks.

Throughout this period, the typical mother cat will be devoted and attentive, alert to every cry from the kittens and completely at the service of their needs. They should not be taken from her for adoption until they are at least eight weeks old, fully vaccinated, litter-box trained, and able to eat a solid diet.

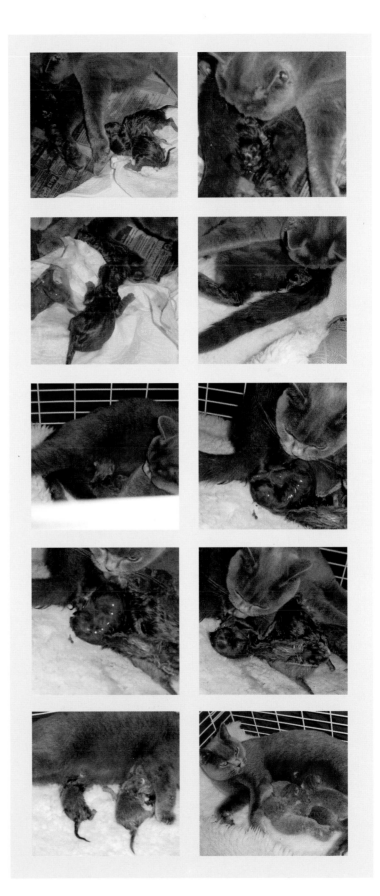

Caring for the Older Cat

At the age of ten years, most cats, just like elderly humans, begin to show signs that their bodies are functioning less effectively than they used to. Decreased hearing, sight, smell, and thyroid function, slower metabolism, a thinner coat, and the appearance of gray hairs, especially around the face, are evidence that your cat is slowing down.

Keep him up to date on vaccination boosters to shore up his immune system and continue to provide the high-quality diet he is used to, but offer him smaller portions three times a day, rather than two larger meals.

Be sure the vet checks his teeth and gums at every visit and continue to clean his teeth regularly at home to prevent tooth loss and periodontal disease.

Since he will be grooming himself less often, it is best to brush him daily, checking at the same time for lumps and other suspicious growths indicative of disease, which require a visit to the vet.

Be sure that his bed is in a warm, dry area, and provide a step stool to help him get up to your bed or to a sunny windowsill. Perhaps you can supplement his time in the sun with a full-spectrum lamp, since window glass prevents beneficial rays from coming through.

🐾 *Ben is beginning to show signs of aging, including taking life at a more mellow pace than he used to. He has some gray hairs around the face, but his coat is in excellent condition for a thirteen-year-old.*

Continue to weigh your cat regularly, since obesity is common—and dangerous—with diminished activity. Be vigilant also about weight loss and a dull or matted coat, which may be signs of hyperthyroidism. This condition is treatable, but not always successfully. I lost my seventeen-year-old, long-haired tortoiseshell, Terra, to this illness about a year after she was diagnosed. But this brings us to topics covered in Chapter 7 on euthanasia and coping with loss.

Feline Habits and Behavior

There is a long history behind most of the habits and behaviors of the domestic cat, many of which baffle the first-time owner and even the seasoned veteran. This section helps to explain, in part, "why kitty does that" by exploring the transition between her forebears—mainly solitary wildcats—and the household pet of today.

Territorialism

When the cat lived in total freedom, it had to defend its own territory from incursions by other animals like or unlike itself, and this ancestral memory is very much alive today. Animal behaviorists have suggested that the cat's territory may be conceived of as three concentric zones.

At the center is its own "sacred space," coinciding with its habitation and represented by the place where it sleeps. The second zone is the area in which it makes its daily or nocturnal rounds, which is also off-limits to intruders. The third zone consists of the large external area that the cat considers its hunting grounds, whether forest or savanna, and which it marks by spraying urine or eliminating feces at intervals corresponding to the parameters of its territory.

In an article entitled "Natural Cat Behavior," the organization Cats International points out that: "The wild counterpart of the domestic

🐾 *The British Shorthair below is part of a multicat household, but he's reserving this space on the sofa as his own personal territory.*

> *"The wildcat is the 'real' cat, the soul of the domestic cat; unknowable to human beings, he yet exists inside our household pets, who have long ago seduced us with their seemingly civilized ways."*
> —Joyce Carol Oates

cat has a large territory, with males patrolling about 150 acres and females, about 15 acres. With the provision of food by humans and the elimination of the mating behavior (by spaying and neutering), the territory of our house cats can shrink to a fraction of the space utilized by their country cousins. . . . There is a limit, however, to what even the most adaptable cat can handle, especially when the already restrictive environment is diminished further by the addition of multiple feline companions. (An average-sized home with three indoor cats has a feline density of about 30,000 individuals per square mile.)"

Given these circumstances, it is a tribute to feline flexibility that the members of most multicat households get along very well. They work out compromises about their boundaries, and sensitive owners will ensure that each animal has its own bed, feeding station, litter box, privacy, and individual attention each day. Occasionally, spats break out, but these are usually resolved between the aggressors before the owner has to intervene with a spray bottle of water or some similarly unwelcome diversion. Yelling or punishing the animals is not only

🐾 *Above, Jessie is keeping a watchful eye at the edge of her "sacred space," or inner territorial zone, where she sleeps.*

abusive, but totally counterproductive: It will only increase intercat aggression and create stress in the relationship between pets and their owners, who are an essential part of their territory.

Curiosity

This feline trait has become synonymous with the cat family, as seen in the proverbial expression, "Curiosity killed the cat." However, this is rarely the case, since cats are so adept at getting themselves out of trouble. Their acute senses, excellent balance, and strong survival instincts serve them well when they ignore the dictates of prudence to satisfy their insatiable curiosity about the environment, possible prey, and other animals—in short,

anything that captures their attention. If they *do* overreach themselves and end up in the top of a tall tree or stuck in the foundations of a house, their loud cries for help will usually summon human aid.

Safety First

The following objects are hazards:

- Shiny objects like pins and needles

- Rubber bands and string (almost impossible to spit out because of the backward-facing barbs on a cat's tongue)

- Thumbtacks

- Cellophane packaging

- Plastic bags that could cause suffocation or choking

- Balls of aluminum foil, which can cause intestinal blockage

You can do your part in protecting your cat from herself by making a checklist like the one shown opposite of objects that pose a threat to her and eliminating them from the environment.

Some pet-care specialists recommend paper bags as an acceptable cat toy, but I've seen several cases in which cats became entangled in the handles of these bags when entering them and panicked, rushing mindlessly around the room or even out of doors, at great danger to

🐾 *Don't expect to keep anything hidden from your kitten unless it's securely locked away. She'll make it her mission to explore every nook and cranny in minute detail.*

themselves and distress to their owners. This temptation to curiosity could, indeed, kill the cat, and should be avoided entirely.

Hunting

Patient, stealthy, and alert, the contemporary house cat is a hunter of rare skill, equal to that of his wild cousins. His principal prey includes mice, rats, birds, and fish, when he can get them, as illustrated in so many cartoons of cats hovering hopefully over the fishbowl.

Mice and birds are probably the most frequent "unwanted gifts" brought home by a cat to show his

hunting prowess, and true animal lovers are between a rock and a hard place in these cases. Most are saddened by the destruction of these little creatures (perhaps the birds more than the mice!), but they know that their pets are driven to hunt, even when well fed, by primordial instincts for which they cannot be blamed.

play of kittens, when they may pounce on a ball (= a mouse), fling it up into the air and leap after it (= a bird), or flip it over the shoulder and spin around to trap it (= a fish). All these special killing actions are programmed into the brain of the kitten, awaiting further development as it matures, and in the meantime revealing themselves as exciting, and highly predictable, play-patterns."

🐾 *Domestic cats retain the hunting instincts exhibited by their wild counterparts. However, for indoor cats, the "prey" is more likely to be a toy, a ball, or a piece of string or yarn than anything that's living and breathing.*

Even a drowsy tabby in a sunlit corner of the yard will be wide awake at the slightest rustle in the grass, either freezing in hopes that the prey will approach, or stalking it for a lethal pounce and a killing bite to the back of the neck. Head-swaying and tail-twitching are signs that an attack is imminent.

The renowned animal behaviorist Desmond Morris describes, in his book *Cat World: A Feline Encyclopedia*, "Three different kinds of 'final strikes,' depending on the type of prey [the cat] is attacking. . . . These three different actions can often be seen in the

Leaping and Climbing

Some breeds, including the agile Siamese, are well known for their amazing leaps to the tops of tall dressers and other challenging heights in and out of doors. These feats often startle visitors, but it is hard to deter the athletic cat from showing off its strength and agility in this way. You are well advised to clear high spaces of bric-a-brac and other decorative features when such a cat is loose in your house.

🐾 *Kittens leap as if to pounce on their "prey," demonstrating an aspect of their hunting instincts (below). One of the reasons cats climb is to escape danger—especially, when indoors, in the form of a boisterous toddler or an overly enthusiastic dog. This action is known as the "flight" response to a threat.*

Author Rodger Wilson tells us that his cat, Hester, has aspirations of this type and "likes to be as high up as she can. Chairs, bookshelves, mantels, even a ceiling fan can become the perfect perch. I think if she were outside, we would find her hanging from a cloud."

As to champion climbers, Desmond Morris reports that: "Perhaps the most remarkable instance of domestic feline climbing ability concerns a female cat in Bradford, Yorkshire [England], in 1980. Attacked by a dog, it climbed seventy feet up a sheer, vertical…wall of a five-story apartment building."

Sleeping

The average full-grown cat spends two-thirds of the day sleeping, in phases that range from the brief, so-called catnap, to periods of light sleep, followed by deep sleep. The latter is characterized by total relaxation, as shown by the animal's lying on its side and exhibiting signs of dreaming—twitching, rapid eye movement, and quivering of ears, paws, or tail. This is typical of much larger feline carnivores, including the lion, which drowses for long periods between its hunting and feeding expeditions.

During deep sleep (the only kind that newborn kittens experience for their first month), the cat's trunk remains immobile

and relaxed, even as its extremities show movement. It may also make involuntary vocalizations in this state—growls, purrs, or indistinct mutterings. Such periods of deep sleep rarely last more than six or seven minutes. The animal then returns to light sleep for thirty minutes or so, when it awakens.

Whether wild or domestic, cats may appear to be sleeping deeply, yet they can still spring into action upon hearing even the slightest sound nearby.

 *Cats learn to groom themselves, and their littermates, at a very early age. If your cat licks you as well as herself, this indicates that she's closely bonded with you and wants to groom you, too—although her rough tongue might seem more like torture than affection to you!*

Washing

The three-dollar word to describe this familiar feline activity is "autogrooming," whereby the cat grooms itself. (When it grooms another cat, it's called "allogrooming.") The latter is seen most often in the early weeks of a kitten's life, when its mother grooms it regularly, and it also occurs between littermates after their first month and between mature cats of the same household as a gesture of friendliness and shared turf.

Feline Facts

🐾 The cat's meticulous grooming has given it a reputation for great cleanliness and even a place in folklore as a weather predictor. Some people believe that if a cat spends a long time washing behind its ears, the weather will be fair. Others, however, believe that the same activity foretells an approaching storm.

The average house cat in good health will groom itself regularly, from face-washing with alternate paws to licking its tail from base to tip. In fact, grooming behavior is a major indicator of your cat's overall well-being. It not only has a calming effect on her, it keeps her skin and coat in good condition.

Her saliva dampens the fur and enables her to "comb" it by licking, which removes dust, small bits of vegetation, and tangles that could become painfully matted. It also improves the insulating qualities of the coat during cold weather and stimulates skin glands at the base of the hairs that improve their waterproofing function during wet weather. Note that older cats and those that have become obese may need extra brushing and combing as their ability to reach various parts of their bodies diminishes.

🐾 *If your cat begins to groom himself more frequently, he may have developed a skin allergy or a flea problem. Excessive grooming can also lead to hair balls and digestive problems.*

Spraying

Unaltered male cats mark their territories by squirting a powerful (and pungent) jet of urine backward onto various features of the environment, from indoor furniture to outdoor fences, tree stumps, and walls. They are especially attracted to places where they or other cats have sprayed in the past, making their rounds in a set pattern and, apparently, gathering olfactory "news" about other cats in the vicinity. This habit is one that can be eliminated, or nearly so, by neutering, which strengthens the argument for surgical sterilization.

Clawing Fabrics and Other Household Items

This unpopular activity is usually referred to as the cat's having "sharpened its claws" on your prized loveseat or table leg. However, it is more accurately described as "stropping," since the claws are not being sharpened like knives to a finer point. Rather, the old claw sheaths are being removed by this tearing action to reveal new claws beneath them.

Done only with the front feet, this behavior also exercises and strengthens the tendons that govern the retraction and protrusion of the claws, which is essential to the successful capture of prey. (The outworn hind-claw sheaths are chewed off by the cat in the course of its regular grooming.) To prevent inadvertent, but very real, destruction to your decor, see page 211 on training your cat to use a scratching post.

> 🐾 *From the age of five months or so, a cat will begin to scent-mark his territory. Stropping, or clawing with the front paws, helps the cat remove its old claw sheaths. Interestingly, it's also a form of scent-marking; there are scent glands in the front paws.*

Grass-eating

This puzzling behavior, which indoor cats often duplicate by chewing on houseplants, has been explained in many ways. Some experts believe that cats use grass as a laxative, to help them eliminate hair balls lodged in their intestines. Others suggest that they eat it to add roughage to their diets, or to relieve stomach irritation. The consensus now is that the juices of grass and similar plants like chives contain folic acid, which is essential to the production of hemoglobin. Since folic acid is absent from an all-meat diet, cats instinctively seek out fresh grasses to obtain it.

For indoor cats, small containers of grasses that sprout readily can be obtained at many pet-supply stores, or through the websites and catalogs listed in the back of this book. For cats that frequent the garden, it is vital to be sure that no potentially poisonous herbicides or other chemicals are used to treat the lawn or flower beds.

Paws for Thought

Some popular houseplants (including poinsettia, above) are poisonous to cats. For a list of harmful plants that must be avoided for your cat's safety, see page 243. Provide your cat with edible grasses (left) if he lives indoors.

Understanding Your Cat's Body Language and Voice

Eye Signals

There are many ways in which your cat signals mood changes and states of arousal visually. For example, if her pupils become much larger within a second or two, she has just seen something that is either intensely appealing or highly threatening to her.

Her eyes will always remain fully open when she is on the alert or when strangers are nearby, but this differs from the behavior called "staring," which is an overtly hostile signal to another animal or to a human. The long, direct stare must always be read as a warning. The degree of eyelid opening or closure has its own significance. Half-closed eyes show that your cat is totally relaxed, while closed eyes indicate either a state of sleep or one of appeasement. During a cat fight, the animal that is losing may signal capitulation by turning away and closing its eyes, much as a defeated wolf offers its throat to the dominant animal in surrender. In both cases, the fight is over.

"And gaze into your gazing eyes,
And wonder in a demi-dream
What mystery it is that lies
Behind those slits that glare and gleam..."
—Lytton Strachey

Ear Signals

Your cat's ears can not only be rotated to improve hearing from various directions, they can indicate its emotional state as well. In the relaxed state, the ears point forward and slightly outward. Twitching of the ears signals that the animal is agitated or conflicted about something in its environment. A cat that is on the defensive displays fully flattened ears, which are pressed tightly against the head to protect them in the expectation of a fight. An aggressive cat that is ready for trouble shows an ear position that is often seen in wildcats—its ears are flattened but not fully rotated. This indicates that the cat is not afraid of a fight and is ready to attack should its opponent make an offensive move.

Half-closed eyes (opposite, above left) are a sign of a drowsy or contented cat, while a quick change in the pupil size of an alert cat indicates her response to the sudden appearance of a threat or potential prey. Twitching ears and rotation of the ears are also clues to a cat's circumstances and behavior.

out at the owner on its way to emergency veterinary care. (This is the sound that none of us wants to hear.)

Fright An alarming, throaty, yowling noise, usually expressed when a cat is cornered by a larger adversary, but serves warning that it will attack no matter what. This is usually accompanied by an arched back, upraised fur, "bottlebrush" tail—all of which are displays that make the cat look larger and fiercer—along with spitting and hissing. (Some authorities suggest that the latter actions resemble the threat of a poisonous snake, which most animals instinctively avoid.)

Voice Signals

Your cat actually has two different vocabularies: the one it uses with its human companions and the other derived from its former life in the wild, which is now used with other animals. Essentially, the domestic cat can be said to express about seven different types of messages, as outlined below:

Contentment This is the purr, which communicates nonhostile intentions between the cat and his human owner and also between, for example, nursing mothers with their kittens. It can also occur when a dominant adult cat approaches a younger cat in a friendly way, or vice versa. This familiar and disarming sound assures all concerned that things are going well.

Welcome This is a soft chirruping sound used by mother cats who want their kittens to follow them or as a greeting when she has been absent. Adult cats often vocalize this "rising trill" when they greet their human owners. It is usually accompanied by the act of winding between the owner's legs and rubbing against them, which is the same type of scent-marking used with other friendly pets of the household.

Pain This distressing cry is heard only when the animal is in great pain and literally screams to express it. If the source of the pain—say, a tail caught in a door—cannot be relieved, the animal should be wrapped in a towel and restrained, to prevent its lashing

"Attention, please!" A whole spectrum of meows, from soft to loud and demanding, will soon become familiar as your pet's expression of his requirements, including his displeasure at the disruption of a fixed routine, like feeding time. An amusing article in the January/February 2003 issue of *Best Friends* magazine, entitled "Meow Mystique," sums up this vocabulary and its effects: "Although they don't communicate in human language, cats are quite adept at manipulating humans to get what they want: namely, food, shelter, and affection. Hundreds of cats' meows were played for human test subjects, who

🐾 *This four-week-old Ragdoll kitten is crying to attract its mother's attention. As the kitten matures, it will learn to make (and recognize) a number of distinct voice signals.*

rated them according to how urgent the call seemed, or how pleasant. Cats clearly got across the message of what they wanted. A rapid, rather distressed meow generally made humans feel like running for the closest can of Fancy Feast. Subtler meows made humans more likely to dole out affection and attention."

Anger When adult cats fight, often over a female in heat, their caterwauling is unmistakably loud and hostile—a cacophony of growls, snarls, wails, and howls that can be heard far and wide. (In my experience, only fighting raccoons can make such alarming sounds, which rise and fall in intensity and ferocity like those of a cat fight.) This explains the many cartoons that depict shoes and other objects flying from the windows of irate people whose sleep has been interrupted by the competition among amorous tomcats. Even two cats engaged in a vigorous fight can make almost enough noise to wake the dead. (Still another reason to keep your cats inside, especially at night.)

Teeth-chattering and clicking sounds These are usually heard when an indoor cat spots a prey animal, like a bird, through the window. It appears to express the frustrated desire to attack the inaccessible prey.

Tail Signals

The tail, as an appendage of balance, also has much to tell us about a cat's shifting moods and intentions.

- The relaxed cat holds its tail curved downward, then rising at the tip.

- When the tail is held erect, the cat is expressing an unreserved greeting to a welcome owner or visitor.

- A female cat in heat signifies her receptivity to the male by holding her tail to one side, which conveys the fact that she can be mounted and will not attack.

- When the cat's tail is lowered and fluffed out, it is fearful. When the tail swings vigorously from side to side, it is about to attack.

- A submissive cat keeps its tail fully lowered and may even, like a dog, tuck it between its hind legs.

🐾 *Most people know that when cat's "wag" their tails, they do so for different reasons than dogs. However, there are a number of tail signals commonly seen in cats that are less widely recognized.*

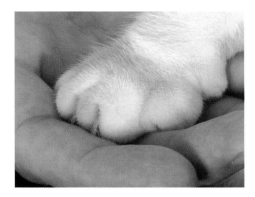

Kneading, or Treading

This activity is seen in newborn kittens that are nursing, and is accompanied by loud purring. With their forepaws, they alternate the kneading action that ensures a steady flow of milk from their mother's nipples. Adult cats often revert to this kittenish behavior when they are seated on their owner's lap and fully content. Unfortunately, their sharp claws can cause serious discomfort, and they are confused when picked up and placed on the floor. At this point, we must remember that we are maternal figures to our pets, since we provide food and other comforts that they experienced in infancy. As Desmond Morris points out, "This is a classic example of the way in which interactions between humans and cats can lead to misunderstandings. Many can be avoided by recognizing the fact that an adult domestic cat always remains a kitten in its behavior to its pseudoparental owner."

Playful Aggression

This behavior is often seen in young, active cats that need outlets for their energy and may show it by chasing, ankle-grabbing, and other undesirable activities. Owners who adopt a kitten may inadvertently contribute to this behavior by encouraging it to chase after or bite at their hands or feet during play. The kitten's milk teeth do not inflict a painful bite, but even an inhibited bite from a full-grown cat is another story.

The principal strategy for preventing playful aggression is to provide your young cat with ample opportunities to play with intriguing toys like those suggested in Chapter 3 and to rotate them once their novelty wears off. You will find that your cat prefers some of these toys to others, and they play an important role in developing her spirit of exploration, investigation, and predation—qualities she would need to ensure her survival under other circumstances.

"Don't Pet Me Anymore" Aggression

Many of us have experienced this confusing behavior, whereby a cat that is being petted suddenly bites or grasps your wrist with its claws. Males are more likely to do this than females, although even the animal behaviorists are unsure why it occurs. Apparently, each cat has its own tolerance for being petted or held, so if your pet begins to display the behaviors outlined on the checklist shown below, respect its boundaries.

"Enough Is Enough"

- 🐾 Restlessness
- 🐾 Tail-twitching
- 🐾 Ears turning back or flicking
- 🐾 Cat's head moving toward your hand

"Telephonitis"

Like children, cats have developed all kinds of ways to forcibly recapture your attention when you're talking on the phone. A few simple deterrents can help improve your interpersonal communications.

One is to keep the telephone area "out of bounds" by not interacting with your pet in any way where you make most of your calls. Another is to hide treats or spread catnip in his favorite play area to distract his attention while you're talking. As a last resort, if he persists in pawing, jumping, or calling to you when you're on the phone, spray him with the dreaded water bottle—sometimes just picking it up will send him running.

I ❤ CATS

6

Basic Care
and Grooming

Here we explore in more detail some of the care-related topics that were introduced in earlier chapters.

Ideally, even as a first-time cat owner, you will feel confident that you can meet the needs of your new companion and have a great deal of fun in the process. Cats are wonderfully entertaining, and many writers and artists have shown their humorous side in such creations as Warner Brothers' *Tom and Jerry* cartoons, Don Marquis's poem "The Song of Mehitabel," and P. G. Wodehouse's *Webster*, who was "very large and very black and very composed. He con-

this is the song of mehitabel
of mehitabel the alley cat
as i wrote you before boss
mehitabel is a believer
in the pythagorean
theory of the transmigration
of the soul and she claims
that formerly her spirit
was incarnated in the body
of cleopatra
that was a long time ago
and one must not be
surprised if mehitabel
has forgotten some of her
more regal manners

—Don Marquis
from, *the song of mehitabel*

veyed the impression of being a cat of deep reserves. Descendant of a long line of ecclesiastical ancestors who had conducted their decorous courtships beneath the show of cathedrals and on the back walls of the bishops' palaces, he had that exquisite poise which one sees in high dignitaries of the Church."

Hopefully, your relationship with your cat will disprove the tongue-in-cheek comment made by author Amy Hempel in *Nashville Gone to Ashes*: "Animals are pure…. There is nothing deceptive about them. I would argue: think about cats. They stumble and fall, then quickly begin to wash—I *meant* to do that. Pretense is deception, and cats pretend: Who, me? They move in next door where the food is better and meet you in the street and don't know your name, or *their* name."

🐾 *As a cat owner, it's your responsibility to protect your pet and safeguard her well-being. At times, this will be a challenge!*

Diet and Nutrition

There is a bewildering variety of both wet and dry foods on the market, and what to feed your cat will depend largely on her age, size, and preferences. Your veterinarian is your best advisor on kitten food, which is specially formulated to meet the kitten's need for extra protein and fat. This does not necessarily imply an expensive brand from the pet store.

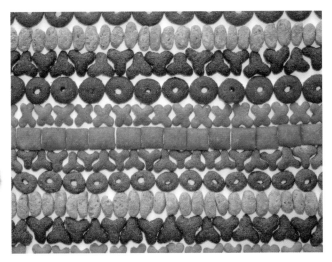

Products available at the supermarket may be quite acceptable, if you read the packaging carefully for statements on nutritional adequacy. If the product states "feeding test," it means that it has been tested on real kittens in a scientific manner and found suitable. The phrase "meets nutritional requirements" means that the manufacturer used a chemical analysis to ensure that the product provides a balanced diet. While it may be entirely acceptable, it has not been analyzed with the help of real-life kittens over a period of time.

Most veterinary nutritionists suggest that a meat source should be at the top of the ingredients list. Labels reading "lamb" or "chicken" suggest a higher grade of food than those in which "by-products" or "meal" predominate. Cats are essentially carnivores, and not all of them can readily digest plant proteins. The latter foods are generally less expensive, but they can prove to be a false economy.

Most authorities caution against giving cow's milk to kittens or adult cats, as they do not have the enzyme necessary to digest the milk sugar, lactose, properly and can develop debilitating diarrhea. When supplementary feeding for a litter that is being weaned is necessary, goat's milk or lactose-free evaporated milk is a better choice.

As the kitten matures, she will express her preference for particular foods. Many owners feed canned food twice a day and keep a continual supply of dry food available in a separate dish, since most cats are nibblers rather than gulpers. Of course, if you have a dog in your household, too, you'll need nimble footwork to keep him from consuming everything you put down for the cat! You can avoid this problem best by providing separate, secure feeding areas for both of your pets.

There are so many varieties of cat food available in supermarkets and pet-supply stores that it can seem difficult to choose what is most appropriate for your pet. Read the nutritional information on the packaging carefully. If you are in doubt, ask your vet to recommend a diet and feeding plan.

Health and Hygiene

As stated in earlier chapters, it is essential to provide easily laundered bedding materials and to keep the litter box clean. In a recent letter to *CatWatch*, the newsletter published by the Cornell University College of Veterinary Medicine, a reader complained that "Mr.

Whiskers keeps 'forgetting' he has a litter box." The editors replied, "Most often, the problem isn't in the cat's mind, it's in his box, which you may have neglected to clean. He also may dislike the litter you're using. As many as 90 percent of cats prefer clumping litter. He may dislike the box itself or its location.

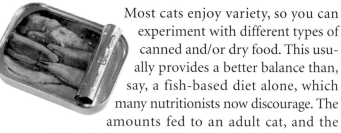

Most cats enjoy variety, so you can experiment with different types of canned and/or dry food. This usually provides a better balance than, say, a fish-based diet alone, which many nutritionists now discourage. The amounts fed to an adult cat, and the nutritional adequacy of her diet vis-à-vis those of a kitten, depend on her size, weight, and level of activity. Kitten food is too rich for the mature cat, and aging cats might require special diets recommended by your veterinarian for a variety of conditions, from cystitis to arthritis. Should your cat reject food for more than forty-eight hours or begin vomiting repeatedly, she should be examined by your vet at once.

🐾 *Most cats enjoy being treated to the occasional dish of salmon or sardines, or other favorites like chicken. However, they'll receive the best all-round nutrition from a regular diet of cat food formulated specially for their own age and activity level.*

Cats don't like dark, smelly bathrooms on noisy streets any more than you or I would. If you give Mr. Whiskers spotless litter and privacy, but the problem persists, the cause could be medical. It would be wise to schedule a physical exam promptly."

In another letter to *CatWatch*, the editors solved a problem baffling a reader who asked why "Sassy insists on plopping her favorite toy right into her food dish." Interestingly, they advised: "Behaviorists believe that most, if not all, play behavior in cats is truly predatory behavior." (More about this later.) "Consequently, a cat chasing a toy, in actuality, is chasing 'prey.' It's reasonable to suspect, then, that Sassy is taking her 'prey' to the place where she normally eats or drinks."

Many knowledgeable sources suggest that you may want to put together a first-aid kit for your special friend, in hopes that you'll never need it. If you do, here's a suggested checklist of what to have on hand:

Better Safe...

- ✔ Sterile gauze pads

- ✔ Cotton balls and/or swabs

- ✔ Hydrogen peroxide for disinfecting cuts or bites

- ✔ Antibiotic lotion

- ✔ A pillowcase or towel to confine your pet for treatment

- ✔ Rubber or latex gloves

- ✔ Penlight for checking eyes, ears, or mouth for injury

- ✔ Heating pad

- ✔ Tweezers

🐾 *Houseplants that are poisonous to cats should be kept well out of harm's way. Remember that high places are usually still within an active cat's reach.*

If your cat is especially inquisitive or dexterous, you may want to provide locks or other deterrents on storage places for poisonous materials like cleaning supplies, antifreeze, pesticides, and rat poison. Be aware also of the danger inherent in open clothes washers and dryers—always check inside before you use these appliances. A list of plants poisonous to cats is included on page 243 of this book. If you grow any of them, hang them high! (The same is suggested for birdcages, so Sylvester doesn't keep Tweety Bird in a state of continual agitation—or worse.)

"Cats don't need our flattery. They know that they're gorgeous and aristocratic, that they're gifted dancers, great batters, admirable vocalists, and accomplished acrobats. We can brag all we want about our cats and they'll just go on doing whatever they've been doing, because cats are really self-employed and don't care if they please the boss or not."

—Michael J. Rosen

Feeling Below Par

🐾 Unusual weight changes

🐾 Lumps, whether hard, soft, or fluid-filled

🐾 Changes in eating or drinking habits

🐾 Head-shaking or ear discharge

🐾 Obvious pain, or avoidance of touch

🐾 Fever

🐾 Bloated stomach

🐾 Listlessness—lack of usual energy

🐾 Pale gums or eye rims

🐾 Breathing difficulties or nasal discharge

🐾 Coughing, or streaming eyes

🐾 Straining to void or defecate

Pet to Vet

It's a rare cat that rushes eagerly into his carrier for a trip to the vet, so you may have to out-smart him to keep him from fleeing the scene. Some people leave the carrier out for a day or two before the prospective visit, giving their pets a chance to refamiliarize themselves with it.

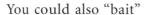

You could also "bait" the carrier by putting a few cat treats inside to see if he'll investigate, then locking the door quickly behind him. Eventually, you may just have to pick him up—with a towel, if necessary—and insert him into the carrier, which should always be placed in the back seat of the

🐾 *Getting your cat successfully into his carrier may turn into a struggle for both of you, unless he's been accustomed to his carrier from an early age.*

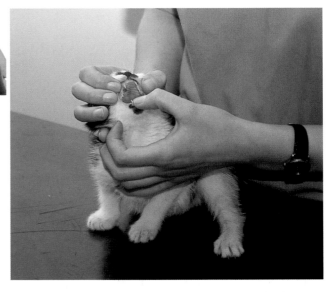

Your kitten may find her early trips to the vet quite stressful, but she will cope better if she's used to being handled and groomed from the beginning. Here, the vet performs routine checks on a kitten for signs of health problems. The first inoculations may be greeted with a yelp, as here, but this is due more to surprise than pain.

car for safety's sake. Even a disgruntled cat that complains all the way to the vet is preferable to one that is trying to help you drive the car or escape through the window.

Some people prefer to see a cats-only practitioner so their pets are not exposed to the stressful sounds and odors of barking dogs. Others prefer a veterinarian who will make house calls, but this is unusual and relatively expensive. Once your cat has received the initial inoculations recommended by your vet and been spayed or neutered, he should not need more than an annual checkup, fecal exam, and booster shots, except in cases of injury or illness. (You may wish to invest in a thermometer for your first-aid kit, as your cat's temperature should never rise above 102.5°F or fall below 100°F.) Your local clinic can show you how to use the thermometer if your pet shows signs of illness (see the caution on page 171).

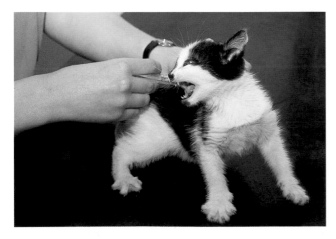

Permanent Identification

In recent years, two forms of permanent identification have become more widely available—tattooing and microchipping. Your veterinarian can advise you on these safeguards against your pet's being lost, strayed, or stolen, since they afford even more protection than the collars and tags mentioned in Chapter 3.

Tattooing is done inside the ear as a series of numbers that are registered with a national pet registry organization. It may be useful to state on your cat's identification tag that he has been tattooed. This may discourage potential thieves, since you will be able to prove ownership. Unfortunately, many cats that are not traceable are stolen for sale as laboratory subjects. (For the same reason, you should guard against advertising cats or kittens in the newspaper as "free." This attracts the same type of people, whose stories can be very plausible.)

Microchipping has gained increasing popularity as a form of permanent identification in recent years. A microchip about the size of a grain of rice can be programmed with an unalterable code number and has the electronic circuitry to send out this unique number. No batteries are involved, and the chip can last up to twenty-five years. Available only through licensed veterinarians for cats at least six months old, the microchip is implanted by injection in the skin below the scruff of the neck. The procedure takes only seconds and the veterinarian scans the microchip before inserting it to confirm the code. Afterward, it is rescanned to verify the code and ensure that it is working.

It is hoped that a universal scanner will soon be developed, but until that time, the microchip serves as a tracking device, or transponder, that sends a signal only when activated by a compatible scanner. (Perhaps you have seen this procedure used for wild-animal research and rescue operations on television or in magazines on natural history.) Some scanners now in use for pet protection can identify chips other than their own, and when a signal is

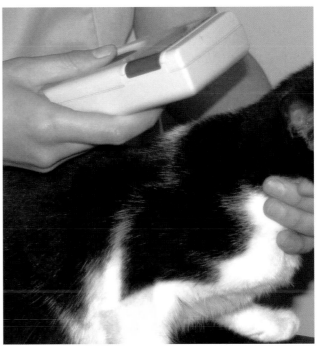

activated, the scanner decodes it and displays the identifying code on a liquid-crystal display window.

According to Kim Campbell Thornton and John Hamil, D.V.M., the authors of *Your Aging Cat:* "There are advantages to listing a microchipped cat with a national registry. These services usually provide twenty-four-hour notification, a tag notifying finders that the cat is microchipped, and instructions on how to contact the registry, and are usually affiliated with a number of shelters across the country. However, even if you choose not to register your cat with one of these organizations, a shelter or laboratory can still locate and notify the veterinarian who implanted the chip."

Given the cat's propensity to escape from the house, this procedure puts her at extreme risk and may have long-term effects on her personality. As Johnson points out, many declawed cats become biters, because they feel anxious about their defenselessness, including the inability to climb to safety. The procedure is already outlawed in thirteen European countries, and in 2003, West Hollywood, California, passed an ordinance banning the declawing of cats. The city council has been researching the legal aspects of enforcement, in hopes of encouraging other municipalities to halt the practice. See page 211 for methods of training your cat to use the scratching post.

Declawing: Increasingly Controversial

Up until recently, many cat owners who intended their pets to remain indoors had them declawed. This practice has become increasingly controversial, for reasons that are clear from the following quotation by Pam Johnson, the author of *Cat Love*:

"Luckily, many vets are against declawing except as a last resort…Rather than trying to put this in delicate terms, I'm going to come right out and tell you that the declawing operation is amputation. It's the equivalent of you having the last joint of all your fingers removed. That's exactly what happens to your cat. Under anesthesia, the last joint of each of her toes is completely removed… Most cats continue to experience pain for a few days after the operation…Once declawed a cat becomes almost totally defenseless, and some people have the hind claws removed in addition, which leaves the cat *completely* defenseless."

Grooming

Your kitten is old enough to go to the groomer after it has completed its vaccinations, and well-trained groomers are your best source of advice on towel or blow-drying, as well as brushing, combing, and nail-clipping. The latter process should be done quickly but reassuringly, with a clipper designed for cats only. This is easily done by pressing gently on each paw pad until the nail protrudes. Trim off only the sharp tips about once a month, or when you see that your cat's claws are catching on its scratching post, and do not cut into the quick, the blood supply that feeds the nail, which will cause pain and bleeding. Have styptic powder on hand in case this happens, but there should be no problem if you are careful. If this process intimidates you, let your vet or groomer take care of it. In many cases, however, good scratching and climbing posts will make nail trimming unnecessary.

Before brushing your cat, check his entire body for any unusual lumps, sores, or even bites from another cat—difficult to detect in a long-haired pet before such a bite abscesses and causes obvious limping or other evidence of injury. Long-haired cats, as mentioned earlier, need daily brushing to prevent mats and tangles (and consequent hair balls) from forming. These can be brushed out painlessly if you secure the hair at the base of the tangle and work toward the skin from the tips of the hair. Short-haired cats also need regular brushing to remove dead hair, especially during the shedding season. A metal comb will help you detect the presence of fleas.

🐾 *Fudge, a short-haired cat, doesn't need daily brushing, but her coat benefits from regular combing to help remove dead hair and to control shedding.*

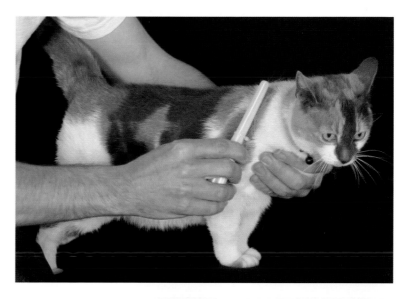

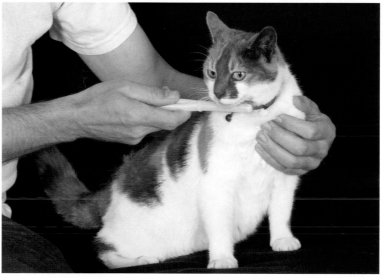

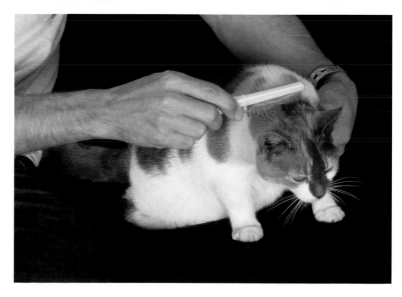

Breeding

We've come a considerable way from the viewpoint expressed by one of humorist P. G. Wodehouse's characters during the early twentieth century. "What I've got against cats," said a Lemon Sour, "is their unreliability. They lack candor and are not square shooters. You get your cat and you call him Thomas or George, as the case may be. So far, so good. Then one morning you wake up and find six kittens in the hat box and you have to reopen the whole matter."

Today the breeding of pedigree cats has become an art and science unto itself, while the random breeding of unsterilized pets is, fortunately, on the wane. As mentioned earlier, cat breeding is probably best left to the professionals, but life being what it is, our household pets or an adopted stray sometimes surprise us with a litter of kittens. Fortunately, there is a chance that good homes can be found for all of them among our friends and neighbors or through contacts at our local veterinarians' offices and pet-supply stores. Even so, spaying and neutering are the best solutions to pet population control—sadly, there are just too many cats.

If you own a pedigree cat, you may have made a contract with the breeder that is designed to protect both of you as well as the kitten you've acquired. A reputable breeder will always tell you whether your choice is a pet-quality or show-quality kitten, according to the prevailing standards. Breeders are quick to point out that not every litter includes only show-quality kittens; in fact, one or two per litter is a high proportion. However, it is wise to go over your kitten's pedigree with your breeder, even if you don't plan to show her. You will find out how to register your purebred and whether or not there are grand champions in her pedigree, which attests to the predictable appearance and temperament resulting from her bloodline.

Should you decide to breed your queen at maturity, you need to see the pedigree of the chosen stud cat, preferably including up to five generations (at least three, if you don't plan to show). A stud fee should be agreed upon in advance, and you may request a free repeat breeding if your queen doesn't conceive or has only one kitten.

Ask the breeder about the color of the stud cat's littermates and the number of champions and grand champions in his pedigree. When you bring your queen for breeding, be aware that she may go out of season due to the stress of the trip. Even if she is still in heat, she should not be put in with the male immediately, but placed in a cage next to his. And be sure that your breeder will witness the matings when they do come together, that is, when your queen begins to relax and to rub up against the bars of the cage nearest the male. Like most females, she may change her mind once put into the cage with him and produce nothing but hisses and growls. The breeder will remove her from the cage until she is

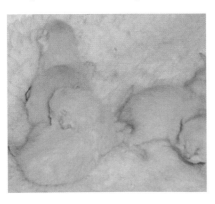

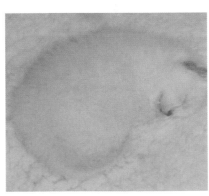

ready to mate, which means you may have to leave her there for a short time. To ensure pregnancy, the pair should be allowed to mate several times over a period of one or two days.

Once your queen has conceived, your veterinarian and, ideally, her original breeder can provide valuable guidance and support throughout her pregnancy, delivery, and mothering period. See the following chapter, "Times When Cats Need Special Care," and be sure that you record the date on which she was bred for your vet's information. In the unlikely event that complications arise, he will have a better idea of how to treat them, and you will be able to plan for the birth of her litter some sixty-three days after the breeding (give or take five days either way). It is interesting to know that the male determines the sex of the kittens and the female determines the number in the litter.

🐾 *Above, a family of Ragdolls: Mother is on the opposite page; father is shown above, left; and the kitten above is a boy from their recent litter, aged thirteen weeks. Below, the litter of Anya and Tam, two British Shorthairs whose offspring include two seal point boys and two seal tortie point girls.*

Training

It is a myth that cats cannot be trained and taught to do things that they might initially resist. Patience and perseverance will enable most owners to teach desirable behaviors like using the scratching post instead of the furniture and becoming accustomed to a leash and/or harness for safe outings away from home. The cat's attitude of independence, as compared to the dog's obvious eagerness to please, has been used to underpin the widespread notion that cats go their own route with total indifference to accommodating their owners. In fact, the opposite is true, despite much humorous comment of the following kind:

> *"Patience was not high on the list of Max's virtues. When he wanted to go outside, Max would look my father straight in the eye and shred a piece of furniture. Replacing furniture was not high on my father's list of priorities. Max was let outside in a hurry."*
> —Paul Meisel

> *"Where most cats are reclusive and cautious, Banshee was a loose cannon; as fast as a shooting star and with the audacity of a kamikaze pilot. Plants, people, furniture, drapes, and other pets didn't stand a chance in her way."*
> —J. C. Suares

We have all laughed about descriptions like these, but we know from experience that the average house cat is very dependent upon its owner's approval and affection and will usually show considerable willingness to learn

Novice owners may be surprised to find that a curious kitten will figure out a way to open the door unless it's securely latched (opposite). Teach your kitten to use the scratching post, as described below, rather than letting him destroy your furniture and walls. Respond to any unwelcome behaviors with a firm "No!"—he won't remember what he did five minutes ago, so correct him immediately to avoid confusion.

basic skills. The feline's innate curiosity also comes into play here, as seen, for example, in teaching your cat to use the scratching post. One of the best ways to do this is to run your fingernails down the post repeatedly while your cat is watching. He will be stimulated by the scratching sound you produce against the sisal, cardboard, or carpet backing and may well emulate your activity and find that it satisfies his need to scratch.

Treating the post with catnip also helps to engage his interest. Rub it into the fabric and around the base every few days. One thing you *don't* want to do is to take his forepaws in your hands and try to "teach" him to scratch—I found this out the hard way. Cats hate any kind of forcing, and my brown tabby was so put off by this attempt that it's taken him years to get the idea that the couch and carpet are not the ideal places to pull off his old claw sheaths.

Fortunately, I don't have a houseful of valuable antiques and rare fabrics. As with children, starting young is a big help in the teaching process. Professional groomers suggest that the best time to give your kitten a first bath is between the ages of two and four months. Read labels carefully

to be sure a cleansing product is made specifically for kittens or cats. And talk to your pet as you bathe it, holding it gently behind its elbows to keep it still while washing with the other hand. Some experts recommend massaging the ear from base to tip, which cats find very calming (more about massaging on page 221).

It has become increasingly common to see cats being walked on a light cord or leather leash, preferably with a harness that will prevent them from slipping out of the collar. A harness of the correct size for your cat is essential and can be obtained from many pet-supply stores, mail-order catalogs, and websites. Introduce it gradually inside the house and put it on for short periods until your pet is accustomed to it. You can then begin leash training—also inside—making short circuits of your house or apartment until your pet feels secure in this new activity. Then you can begin making short for-

ays outside in your garden or to a local park. Most cats love the enticing scents of the outdoors and the feeling of grass under their feet and will soon look forward to these outings. (Remember, though, if you have a Sphynx cat, with almost no fur, it cannot be exposed to direct sunlight.)

Opposite, above: Kittens can be distracted from many of their activities, including the ones you want to prevent them from engaging in, by the temptation of mealtime or a special treat.

Most cats will accept a harness and leash if introduced to the harness gradually, and, preferably, at an early age. This is best learned indoors and "practiced" for some time before you venture out.

behavior that your kitten will need as a healthy, functional adult. Play on her own, or with other pets, teaches her about the environment and allows her to test her strength as she grows. Here she takes turns being the hunter or the "prey," developing motor skills that are enhanced when you take an active part, too. She also learns which objects are appropriate for play, like a catnip-scented toy mouse, and which are not, like your ankles, legs, and fingers.

Playing with Your Cat

A variety of toys that your furry friend might enjoy was suggested in Chapter 3, some of them to be played with alone, and others, with you. Interactive play with your kitten or cat is very important to the bonding process, which, ideally, begins with social play among her littermates and continues into object play

with toys, which enhances mental and physical development.

As with a human infant, play helps lay the foundation for skills and

Animal behaviorists indicate that play is even more important to some cats than to others. If the cuddly Persian or Exotic Shorthair doesn't get enough interactive play with her owner, she tends to become depressed, while the very active Siamese becomes nervous and tense with pent-up energy in the absence of play.

In an article entitled "Acting Class" (*Cats U.S.A, 2001 Annual*), Peggy Scott describes veterinarian-recommended games that will help turn your kitten into an "all-star" cat. They agree that "a toy that just sits there" has limited appeal com-

Feline Facts

🐾 A pregnant female cat will often carry a small, soft toy around in her mouth, indicating that she is rehearsing for motherhood.

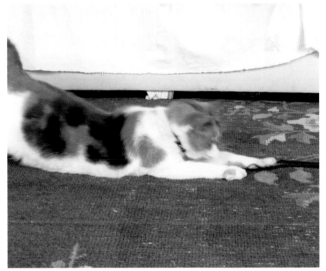

pared to one that flies, hops, rolls, or otherwise entices in the manner of live prey. A particular favorite is a fishing-pole toy with a swivel where the string and the feathers connect, called "Da Bird." When you wave the pole, the feathers spin to resemble the look and sound of a bird in flight. Keep the game interesting by dragging the feathers along the floor or waving them in the air, so when your kitten does pounce on the prey, she has "stalked" it successfully.

Small moving objects always attract a cat's attention. Here, Nick is about to start on Ben's grooming routine, but Ben's decided it's playime!

Another ploy is to cut various-sized holes into a cardboard box, then put some table tennis balls and other toys on the floor and place the box over them upside down. Paw-eye coordination comes into play as your pet reaches through the holes to swat at or drag out the toys.

Should you get tired before your feline friend, you can always hang a furry bug or bird on elastic in an open doorway and turn a small fan on it to make it move. Let it dangle several feet about the floor and watch your kitty move in for the kill. No doubt, you will find or can make other toys that will provide hours of stimulating play and real entertainment for you and your pet.

Traveling with Your Cat

Assuming that you have a secure carrier of the right size, as discussed in Chapter 3, a few simple precautions will make traveling less stressful for both you and your cat. Your carrier should have your name, address, and phone number on it, and your leash and harness (also with identification) will make it possible to make periodic stops for a walk in safe, quiet areas.

The experts advise that you should bring your own cat food *and* water with you, since cats are susceptible to changes in water, just as many people are. Keep a thermos of cool water on hand and offer it in small quantities in the water container. Your cat should be fed at least six hours before departure to prevent any stomach upset. Before leaving on a long car trip, accustom your pet to short trips away from home so that he is less likely to become agitated.

Opinion is mixed on the use of tranquilizers for cats (*only* as prescribed by your vet). Some animals may benefit from them; others will become accustomed to travel through gradual acclimation to journeys. Remember to be calm when putting your pet into the carrier, head first. Your state of mind will have a calming—or an unnerving—effect on him.

For long car trips, you may wish to use a cage large enough to accommodate a small litter box. The dry food your cat is accustomed to is your best bet for travel, so you don't have to deal with opening cans and trying to store leftovers, especially in hot weather.

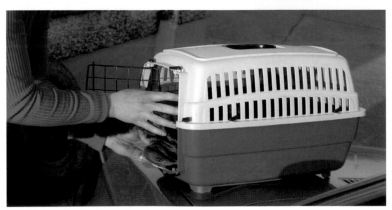

WARNING: Under no circumstances should you leave an animal in a parked car during warm or hot weather or in direct sunlight. Temperatures climb rapidly in this small space, even if you leave the windows open, and can rapidly become life-threatening. Many animals have died of heatstroke in this way.

Should you be traveling by air, get permission in advance to bring your cat on board in a carrier small enough to fit beneath your seat (17 x 12 x 8 in.). Many airlines require a written health certificate and proof of vaccinations, and there may be an extra charge for bringing your cat into the cabin. If you must ship him in the cargo area, have a very sturdy, ventilated carrier lined with newspaper or a towel and posted with his identification and a label reading "LIVE ANIMALS." If possible, book a direct flight for the shortest possible travel time, and don't feed him within six hours of departure.

If you plan to travel by train or bus, be sure you're allowed to bring your cat. Very few bus lines permit this, and many trains don't allow animals on board either. Foreign travel involves numerous regulations, including quarantines of various lengths for some countries and stringent requirements for proof of immunization, written health certificates, and so on. Several helpful websites on traveling with your cat are listed at the end of this book.

🐾 *Left: Placing a cat in his carrier. It's as simple as it looks here—as long as he's used to it. If he struggles, you may need to wrap him in a towel first so that you don't get scratched.*

Brushing Your Cat's Teeth at Home

Twenty years ago, the idea of brushing a cat's teeth probably hadn't been thought of, and if it had, it might have raised gales of laughter. Modern veterinary practice has shown us how important feline dental care is for your cat's overall health and well-being, especially as she ages. Certain dental conditions can cause life-threatening diseases, including

infection and organ failure. Even so, a recent Gallup survey shows that only one in five owners brushes his cat's teeth, and only 63 percent of owners have their cats' teeth professionally cleaned.

If your cat has bad breath, it is the result of bacterial overgrowth in the mouth, which can be arrested by antibiotics, but not cured, except by treating the underlying cause of infection. Your veterinarian can diagnose and treat such causes once they've developed, but preventive care at home is a valuable adjunct to professional dental exams and cleaning.

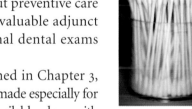

As mentioned in Chapter 3, toothbrushes made especially for cats are now available, along with special toothpaste. Gauze pads, cotton swabs, and finger toothbrushes can also be used to remove plaque at home. Ideally, home dental care should start when your cat is a kitten, but it can be introduced—gradually—in adulthood as well. Daily brushing may not be practical, but three times a week is a good norm.

First, touch your cat's teeth without trying to open her mouth. Over a period of weeks, begin to pull back her lips until she is accustomed to it. Then hold her securely in one arm and begin brushing her teeth with either a toothbrush, gauze pads, or a cotton swab. If she objects to the feline toothpaste, there are a variety of liquids, gels, sprays, and powders to try instead. Eventually you will find the right technique and products to make her dental care part of her regular grooming routine.

Keeping Your Cat Fit

A weekly grooming routine, which provides the opportunity for a quick physical exam, will help keep your pet in top condition. You may wish to invest in a fold-away grooming table with a nonskid surface, especially if you have more than one cat or your grooming will include preparations for showing.

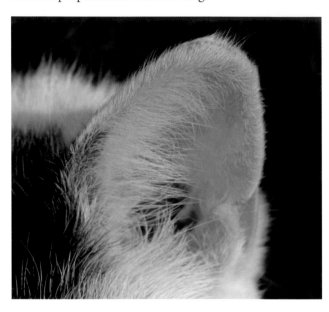

In either case, make a regular practice of examining his head first. Are his inner ears pink and healthy-looking, or are they red and inflamed? Are black particles visible, indicating the presence of mites? Any of these conditions should alert you to the need for a trip to the veterinarian.

Your cat's eyes and nose should appear shiny and free of discharge, and his mouth should be free of lesions, lumps, and tartar buildup. Now is the time to make sure you adhere to your regular routine of brushing his teeth, as described on page 219. His gums should be pink; pale gums may indicate the onset of anemia and other treatable diseases. Note that kittens normally have twenty-six teeth and adult cats have thirty.

Feline Fitnessentials

- ✔ Nutritious food

- ✔ Fresh water daily

- ✔ A personal bond of love and affection

- ✔ Exercise and play

- ✔ A clean, safe environment

- ✔ Regular grooming

- ✔ A predictable routine

Massaging Your Cat

Pet massage has become an increasingly useful technique, not only for bonding with your cat (or dog), but to facilitate recovery from illness or injury and improve the flexibility of aging animals. As with humans, massage stimulates blood circulation, especially to the limbs, increasing the flow of oxygen to the tissues. Skeletal muscles relax, reducing pain where it is present and alleviating muscle spasms.

A good animal-massage therapist or homeopathic veterinarian can teach you the technique in a couple of sessions, and you can then massage your pet at home, when appropriate. Be aware, though, that some conditions rule out massage, including those listed at right.

Be gradual in introducing the massage process to your cat, until he becomes familiar with it. A few minutes at a time is enough in the beginning. And be aware that many cats dislike having their stomachs or their paws touched, which gives them a feeling of vulnerability. You're the best judge of what your cat will allow at the outset. Here are the suggested steps to follow:

How to Massage Your Cat

😺 Stroke your cat gently.

😺 Using a circular motion, start behind his head and massage his neck with your fingertips. Place your thumb in one spot and anchor your hand with it, then move your fingers in a circular motion, pivoting on your thumb. Each time you do it, you move your fingers around in a clockwise fashion, about a quarter turn each time. Then move your hand less than an inch and continue the process, moving a little farther down each time.

😺 Gradually work your way down his back to the tail (which is part of the spine) and to the paws.

😺 Watch your cat carefully to be sure he is enjoying the massage, and stop if he shows signs of discomfort or that he's had enough.

😺 Follow the guideline that applies in all interactions with your pet: The calmer you are, the more relaxed he is likely to be.

Caution—When Not to Massage:

- ✔ When fever is present
- ✔ If limbs are swollen, sprained, or fractured
- ✔ In cases of shock or heatstroke
- ✔ When cancer has been diagnosed
- ✔ In cases of ruptured vertebral disks

Nursing a Sick Cat

Should your cat suffer an illness or injury, be sure that you understand the veterinarian's instructions before you take him home from the hospital. Prescribed medications may include pills or liquids, administered by mouth or plastic syringe, as described below.

The first order of business, especially if you have a multicat household, is to confine the patient to a separate room for rest and quiet. The room should be warm and free of drafts. You can use a cardboard box with an opening cut into it, lined with newspaper and towels, and with a hot-water bottle. A litter box with low sides placed nearby and a small bowl of water complete the sickroom's furnishings. Your vet will advise you on what to feed the convalescent, and you'll want to offer small amounts at a time.

Some owners are daunted by the prospect of pilling their cats (opposite page), but this is relatively simple once you've mastered the basics. The procedure is more reliable than trying to "disguise" the pill in a small pellet of food, which works better with dogs, who tend to gulp. In my experience, the cat will detect the odor of the pill and eat carefully around it, leaving a wet and unusable bit of medication in the bowl.

If you are relaxed about administering medications, your patient will probably be more relaxed, too. In cases of liquid medication administered by mouth with a plastic—*not glass*—syringe, if she becomes panicky, put the medication aside until later; if she breathes in as you administer it, the liquid could be aspirated into her lungs. Sooner or later, the recommended dosages will be given as prescribed, with minimal stress to you and your pet.

Some holistic health-care professionals now suggest various herbal remedies for their feline clients—a relatively recent development that would warrant a book of its own. In fact, numerous books have been written on this subject, some of which are listed on pages 245 and 250. Should you find such natural remedies at your pet-supply store, be sure to check them with your veterinarian before giving them to your cat. As with humans, some herbal compounds may conflict with other medications that have been prescribed. Other tried-and-true herbs like catnip and specially grown "cat grass" for indoor munching can be used safely in almost all circumstances.

How to Give Liquid Medication

1. Tilt the cat's head back slightly after immobilizing her (with a towel if necessary) in an upright position.

2. Place the plastic syringe in the side of her mouth, where the cheek pouch is.

3. Administer the liquid in small amounts, letting her swallow each time.

Caution—Administer only a small amount of medication at a time, or the liquid will leak out of her mouth, or, worse yet, she could inhale it.

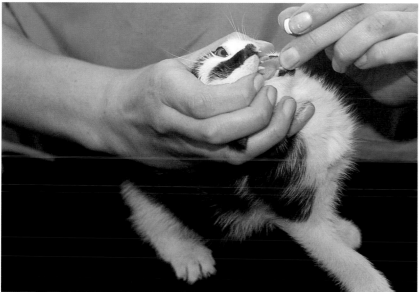

How to Give a Pill

1. If you're dealing with a kitten or a "struggler," you may have to wrap her in a towel first.

2. Grasp the upper jaw firmly.

3. Press gently on the lower jaw to open her mouth. Alternatively, open the mouth by pressing gently on either side of the hinges of the jaw.

4. Slip the pill onto the base of the tongue as far back as possible.

5. Close the mouth gently, but firmly.

6. Hold the jaws shut.

7. Tilt the head back and stroke the throat to encourage the cat or kitten to swallow.

8. She will swallow reflexively.

Caution—Attempt this only if you know the cat isn't aggressive.

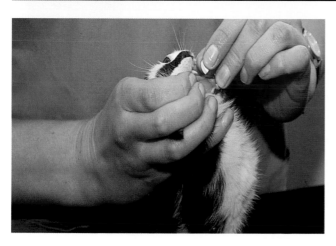

I ♥ CATS

7

Times When Cats
Need Special Care

During Pregnancy

Like all female mammals that breed intermittently, the cat has a reproductive cycle that consists of several phases:

- Anoestrus, during which she will have little or no sexual activity
- Proestrus, the period before coming into heat, which usually lasts several days
- Oestrus, the period during which she is in heat and will mate voluntarily (usually five to eight days).

Like all of us, there are times when your cat needs special care, including pregnancy, birth, early motherhood, and older age. If you have read this far, you are willing and able to provide this kind of care when the need arises. And since a cat's life span is so much shorter than a human's, the time will probably come when *you* need extra help—in making the difficult decision to let your beloved companion go, in cases of incurable illness or injury, and in the aftermath of grieving. Only you will know when the time has come to begin again by enriching some small animal's life, and your own, with the gift of unconditional love.

Since you know your own cat better than anyone, you can monitor her well-being by staying alert to changes in her behavior and appearance. No matter how attentive you are to your pet's needs, though, there will be times when you need help or advice from your veterinarian.

When the cat comes into heat, her behavior is markedly different from the norm. She will appear nervous, caterwaul often, and sometimes crouch, flattening her back and arching her pelvis upward. As hormonal changes increase, she will roll on the floor and rub up against people. Eventually, she kneads with her hind legs and lifts her tail to the side, showing that she will allow the male to penetrate her.

When mating does occur, it looks more like a battle than a romance. The male cat sniffs the female's genital region while she is crouching, then he bites her loose neck fur to mount her.

🐾 *Feline pregnancy is difficult to detect in the early stages. This queen isn't yet visibly pregnant at three weeks (opposite, below), but her nipples are just beginning to enlarge (right, detail below), in preparation for lactation.*

Penetration lasts only a few seconds, ending in a coital scream from the female, who breaks the male's hold by turning and striking him with her paws. Ejaculation and ovulation are simultaneous, and if the female breeds with more than one male, her litter may be fathered by different sires. If there is only one male involved, when breeding is done deliberately to produce a pedigreed litter, the pair may couple from five to ten times within a brief period. In other cases, male and female must be left together for several days before mating occurs.

Before you decide to breed your cat (or should she escape from the house while in heat), it is important to visit the vet to make sure she is up to date with her vaccinations and free of any parasites that could be transmitted to her kittens. No female cat should be allowed to breed until she is fully mature—around twelve months old—because premature breeding may affect her growth.

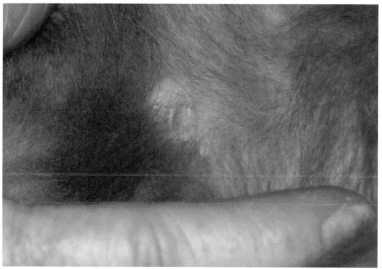

Feline Facts

🐾 A female cat, especially one used for breeding, is called a queen. Breeders refer to their male cats as studs. Desmond Morris suggests that the term "queen" became popular because of the way a female cat in heat "lords it over her males . . . [who] must gather around her like a circle of courtiers, must approach her with great deference, and are often punished by her in an autocratic manner."

The early signs of pregnancy include an unusual amount of licking at the stomach and genital areas, and at about three weeks, enlargement of the nipples, which begin to turn pink. Even an outdoor cat should be kept inside throughout the gestation period, which usually lasts from sixty-three to sixty-five days. Your cat needs moderate exercise during her pregnancy, but do not allow her to jump onto high places. If there are children in the house, be sure that they don't pick her up, since she could miscarry if she fell.

At about six weeks, her abdomen will be visibly swollen and she may have difficulty grooming herself because of her size. You can help by combing and brushing her a

No-nos:
Salami
Pepperoni
Bacon
Lunch meats

OKs:
Tablespoon of yogurt
Small piece of mild cheese
Cantaloupe ball

little each day to keep her coat conditioned. If she has been eating good food with highly digestible protein, you may want to divide it into three portions, rather than two, and increase the quantity gradually during the second month—up to 25 percent.

Pam Johnson, the author of *Cat Love*, advises: "If you haven't been feeding good-quality food, then you'd better start now.... There are commercial foods available for pregnant and lactating cats. You can get them at pet-supply stores or from your vet. I strongly recommend that you do this, because it's the best way to ensure your cat is getting enough protein for herself and her fetuses." Johnson also recommends a checklist (above) of dos and don'ts in the way of treats for your pregnant cat (or any cat).

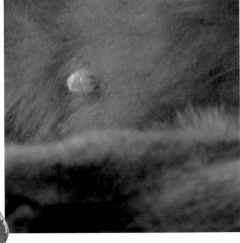

Details on birth and newborn kittens are given in Chapter 5 in the time line section. Be sure that your veterinarian is aware of your cat's due date in case any complications arise. If you are a novice midwife, it's also a good idea to have a more experienced friend at your side.

🐾 *From about six weeks into her pregnancy, the mother-to-be will begin to slow down. She's visibly large by now, and her nipples are prominent. Show her the whelping box when she's within a few days of her due date.*

and then tapered off during the next two to four weeks as she regains her normal weight. One of these recipes (called "Eating for Six") is prepared as follows:

> 2/3 cup cooked chicken, chopped
> 1 teaspoon mayonnaise
> 2 tablespoons steamed vegetables, chopped
> 1 teaspoon steamed bone meal

In a bowl, combine the chicken, mayonnaise, and vegetables. Stir in the bone meal and serve. *Yield: 1 meal; 175 calories.*

The "Queen Mother"

Once all the kittens are safely delivered, the mother will need to rest and should be left in a quiet, darkened room with her newborns. Light food, clean water, and her litter box should be on hand so she will not have to go far from the kittens. A queen who was well fed during pregnancy should be able to nurse an average litter of four to five offspring without difficulty. However, if the litter is unusually large or the mother was adopted as a malnourished stray (see below), she may need help in the form of a vet-recommended supplement that aids milk secretion.

During lactation, your cat will need even more food than she did during pregnancy—say, 200 percent versus 125 percent. In *The Cat Lover's Cookbook*, Franki B. Papai presents eighty-five veterinarian-approved recipes for various stages in your cat's life. For the nursing mother, he recommends a calorie-rich diet to be fed until the kittens are weaned,

Even those who are not avid cat lovers will concede that the female cat is a devoted and courageous mother. A moving tribute to this devotion was inscribed in a London church after World War II to honor a mother cat that survived the Blitz:

pose, as newborn kittens are unable to digest it, so professional advice is needed here. Note also that only the person or persons whom the mother trusts should undertake to bottle-feed the kittens. If they are touched by strange hands, she may be disturbed by the unfamiliar odor and refuse to nurture them herself. Or she may move them from place to place in search of security.

Milk substitutes should be offered to the kittens at a temperature of 100°F, and the "foster mother" should allow the kitten to suck on its own, without forcing it, which could result in suffocation. As with a human infant, when the animal falls asleep or emits bubbles of milk from its mouth that indicate it is no longer sucking, it has had enough.

"On Monday, September 9, 1940, she endured horrors and perils beyond the power of words to tell. Shielding her kitten in a sort of recess in the house (a spot she selected only three days before the tragedies occurred), she sat the whole frightful night of bombing and fire, guarding her little kitten. The roofs and masonry exploded, the whole house blazed, four floors fell through in front of her. . . . Yet she stayed calm and steadfast and waited for help. We rescued her in the early morning, while the place was still burning, and by the mercy of Almighty God she and her kitten were not only saved, but unhurt."

🐾 *If you need to handle newborns, you must respect the mother's natural protective instincts and only approach with the utmost care.*

Should your cat need help feeding an unusually large litter, specially designed bottles or droppers marked with measurements can be used to hand-feed milk substitutes, recommended by the veterinarian, to be sure that the kittens are getting all the nutrition they need. Cow's milk cannot be used for this pur-

Should you take in a pregnant stray cat, the odds of a healthy litter are much smaller, and the mother herself may be at risk. In his teens, my son brought home a stray cat we named Sarah, which had already delivered one kitten in a neighbor's car. We prepared a birthing carton for her and put it in his closet, after offering food and water. The mother was very gentle and grateful, and during the night, delivered two more kittens. Several days later, we brought her and the kittens to the vet and found that all of them were infested with fleas and weakened by malnutrition during her pregnancy.

tails was inadequate. Their tails and hind feet were becoming necrotic, and we had to put them down. It was a tearful day, but we took comfort in the fact that they had received the best possible care during their brief lives, and that Sarah—barely out of kittenhood herself—was taking on new strength each day. Eventually, she grew into a beautiful, silver tabby, devoted to everyone in the family and especially to Eric, her rescuer.

The vet and his staff were very solicitous; they prepared the mildest possible flea dip for Sarah and the kittens, which would otherwise have died outright, and sent us home with special food, bedding, and anything else that would build up their strength. Sarah was a devoted mother, and she began to thrive with good, loving care, but as the weeks went by, it became apparent that the kittens had congenital problems as a result of her deprived circumstances during pregnancy.

When they should have begun to walk, they were very unsteady on their feet, and another visit to the vet disclosed that the blood flow to their hindquarters and

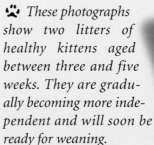

🐾 *These photographs show two litters of healthy kittens aged between three and five weeks. They are gradually becoming more independent and will soon be ready for weaning.*

Your Aging Cat

It's hard to believe that your cat has become a senior citizen by the age of ten, but with good care and attention to subtle changes in his appearance and behavior, he can prosper for years to come. Key to his well-being are the maintenance of a healthy, usually lower-calorie diet, moderate exercise, and adherence to the basic care and grooming regime described in the previous chapter. Regular at-home and professional checkups, including dental health, are more important than ever, along with awareness of the standard signs of aging.

Signs of Aging

- Dry fur and/or flaky skin
- Worn, yellowing, or missing teeth
- Weight loss or gain
- More frequent urination or defecation
- Diminished vision or hearing
- Thinning coat
- Lethargy
- Stiff joints or loss of agility
- Loss of appetite or a marked increase in appetite
- Unusual lumps or sores

As your cat's metabolic rate slows down, he becomes susceptible to many conditions experienced by humans, including diabetes, kidney disease, arthritis, anemia, and cancer. Early detection is your best defense, as well as continuity of care with a veterinarian who knows your cat's history. It is very useful to keep a "Pets" file that chronicles each cat's history of immunization, illness, or injury over the years. See also page 251 of this book, "My Cat's Record," in which you can log such information. These records are extremely helpful to a new veterinarian should you relocate.

tabby kittens that had been abandoned. The local vet determined that they were in good health, and my friend adopted them in the belief that her old friend was about to pass away.

Aggie was outraged! She picked up her bed and walked to put these upstarts in their place. First she hissed and growled at them from behind closed doors, then began chasing them all over the house and cuffing them whenever they took liberties with her. The kittens are fully grown now (half again her size), but they've never questioned her status as "top cat" and all three sleep together on my friend's bed, with full deference to Aggie's place of honor.

Paws For Thought

🐾 Another variation on the theme of old cat/new cat has been described by author, illustrator, and cat lover James McMullan:

"It is now two months since we introduced Wendy the kitten to our fourteen-year-old Burmese, Groucho. Wendy has the upper hand. She runs about where she wants to, poops in Groucho's private litter, and sleeps near him (though she's careful not to touch him). Even if Groucho seems to have lost something of his self-esteem, in the mornings he moves his arthritic legs fast enough to catch Wendy."

There may also be a definite plus side to your cat's mature years. Many people find that their pets mellow with age, becoming less fearful of strangers and changes in routine such as traveling. They may also rise to the challenge in the face of a new pet. A good friend was grieving over what seemed like the imminent demise of her sixteen-year-old, black-and-white cat, named Aggie, when a neighbor found two orange

🐾 *An older cat will probably develop dental problems. Watch for signs of abscesses and gum problems, and gradually alter his diet so he has soft, rather than crunchy, food.*

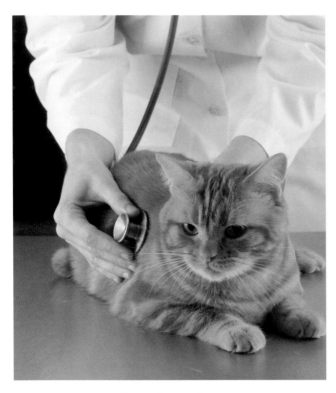

If your cat is terminally ill or suffering from a painful condition, your vet will help you make an informed assessment as to the prognosis and his quality of life.

Letting Go

When the time comes when no amount of love and care can restore our pet's health and quality of life, we hope for the courage to make the right decision on her behalf. Our veterinarians can help us with an honest assessment of her prognosis and the options available, but we are the only ones who can choose to let our companion go without further suffering. This may be the last loving act we can do for her.

As you may know, euthanasia is a quick and painless procedure. The veterinarian prepares an intravenous injection of concentrated anesthetic that brings unconsciousness in ten to twenty seconds. If you wish, your pet can be tranquilized immediately before the injection. There may be brief tremors or gasping as the medication takes effect, but this does not indicate fear or pain. These are simply signs that the muscles are going limp as the animal's life leaves its body.

If euthanasia seems inevitable, there are other matters to consider. It is important that the whole family be involved in the decision, since the pet is a member of the family. Should you, as the primary caregiver, take her to the veterinarian or (if there are no young children there) have the procedure done at home? Should you stay until the end or will this be too much for you? Should you have a friend with you, either at home or at the clinic? Many people have found this to be a comfort.

You may wish to bury your pet at home, where municipal regulations permit this, or have her cremated and bury or scatter the ashes in a favorite place where you spent time together. (Many bereavement counselors suggest that the ashes be disposed of in this manner, rather than kept, in order to help put closure to the loss.) There may well be a pet cemetery nearby, should you decide to take this option. In either case, many people find comfort in marking their pet's resting place with a simple stone or a favorite plant. Others prefer to have their veterinarian dispose of the body.

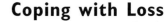

The right decision is the one that is appropriate to the person or family involved. What matters most is unanimity on the matter of putting a beloved animal beyond the reach of pain or incapacitation and the realization that loving memories are an imperishable bond and a source of enduring gratitude.

Coping with Loss

Not everyone is aware that losing a beloved pet can be as painful as losing any other family member. Some people will probably not understand the depth of your grief, but you need to mourn and to honor that need. Be open about your feelings, and don't hold them in—unless with those who will tell you "It's only a cat." Many friends will understand your grief and help support you through the experience.

A bereaved pet owner wrote a letter to the editor of *Cat Fancy* magazine (June 2002) in response to an article on grief in the March issue. She reported that she had gone on-line for support and "found wonderful people who had just gone through losing a pet or were in the same place I was—grieving. It has been almost two years now, and I still e-mail one wonderful woman who has helped me through the grief, and I have helped her through the loss of her second beloved cat."

🐾 *Many people find it especially difficult to see their children coping with the loss of a beloved pet. It is likely that they'll fare better if you are open, not evasive, with them.*

Other resources include pet loss support programs at veterinary clinics that have a grief counselor on staff and universities that teach veterinary medicine and may provide counseling by phone. You may also find a local group or a website like the Association for Pet Loss and Bereavement (see page 245), whose mission statement reads:

"The APLB helps bereaved pet owners find appropriate counseling, personal supportiveness, and reading material. In serving that urgency, this unique organization functions as a clearinghouse for *all* information on this subject. We will continually upgrade and publish

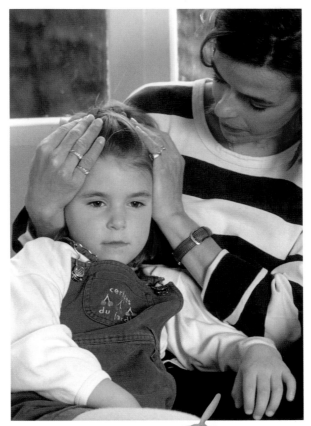

a comprehensive registry of therapies and counselors in this field, according to geographic location. Through the magic of the Internet, this listing is rapidly expanding, worldwide."

If you have children, don't be vague and evasive about the disappearance of the family cat. Cover-ups like "Boots went away" will only confuse them, or perhaps make them feel guilty if they weren't always good to their pet. Their feelings, too, need to be honored by telling them the truth. Perhaps you could help them make a picture album of Boots, or put his picture among the other family photographs as a memorial. You may also wish to pack things like his dishes and his collar in a special box to be kept with his name on it.

In a moving article for *Best Friends* magazine (November/December 2002), Linda Miller describes the loss of both her elderly cats within a few months of each other: "Daisy Mae, [a calico kitten adopted from a neighborhood litter] was a very spunky, affectionate thing who became inseparable from Cochise [the stray white cat that she had taken in the previous year]. His name means "the Peacemaker," because he always sought to intervene in conflicts between other pets and even people in the household." Despite her grief, the author found deep gratitude in remembering how the two friends had "brought me so much joy, comfort, and gentle lessons in living. Daisy taught me to meet life, no matter what it brings, with gusto and spunk, and to love every minute one has on this earth. Cochise taught me to meet each moment of life with a sweet acceptance and deep love, and to make love the most important thing in each and every day."

When to Adopt Again?

Once more, you are the only person who will know the answer to this question when the time comes. Many of us have said, "I can't go through this again," only to find that we cannot do without a pet in our lives.

Sometimes, a new cat will turn up when we least expect her, to help bridge the gap created by loss. In other cases, after an interval of grieving, our heart tells us that "It's time," and we choose another cat—perhaps of the same breed from a reputable cattery or perhaps from a local shelter or animal-rescue group. In either case, we are saying "yes" to life.

If you had more than one pet, the other(s) will undergo a period of mourning, too. Many people who are not animal lovers do not understand the depth of the attachments formed among them and how important it is to respect their process as well. And when the new cat is introduced, it would be unfair to compare him or her to your deceased pet. Undoubtedly, the new arrival will have its own unique temperament, preferences, and engaging qualities. As you know, this is not a matter of replacing a loved animal as one would a kitchen appliance.

As you begin to know your new pet and become involved with meeting its needs and making it comfortable, the grief process is eased by a feeling of usefulness and a growing bond with your new kitten or cat. Many people prefer to adopt a mature animal, or one with a health problem that requires special care. In either case, it is likely that this pet would remain homeless or perhaps be destroyed. If you have the time and resources to make this choice, you will probably never regret it. Even so, it will not erase the memory of its beloved predecessor.

Pet was never mourned as you,
Purrer of the spotless hue,
Plumy tail and wistful gaze
While you humored our queer ways,
Or outshrilled your morning call
Up the stairs and through the hall—
Foot suspended in its fall—While, expec-
   tant, you would stand
Arched to meet the stroking hand;
Till your way you chose to wend
Yonder to your tragic end.

—Thomas Hardy, *from*
"Last Words to a Dumb Friend."

8

Cat Shows, Resources, and Further Information

Cat Shows

According to Carolyn Osier, who is an all-breed judge for the Cat Fanciers' Association and owner of the Wil-o-Glen Cattery for award-winning Abyssinians, the world's first-ever cat show was arranged by Englishman Harrison Weir. He was an all-around animal lover and an authority on such disparate species as felines, racehorses, and poultry (on which he wrote the definitive book of the nineteenth century). When London's famous Crystal Palace opened, Weir had the idea of holding a cat show

there. The year was 1871 and his friends laughed aloud at the notion of "people coming to see ordinary cats," but Weir's proposal turned out to be an inspiration.

There were 160 entries in the show, which, as local newspapers reported it, included "Siamese cats; soft, fawn-coloured creatures with jet black legs; a Persian, direct from Persia [!]; a native of the Isle of Man, with the usual Manx absence of tail." The show attracted such a flood of visitors that it was often hard to see the cats. According to Ms. Osier's same article for *Cat Fancy* (July 2002), "Soon shows were held all over the world and people started keeping records of their breedings, marking the beginning of pedigreed cats and identifiable breeds."

Some cat owners are unaware that you need not have a pedigreed cat to compete in a show. The category "Household Pets and Mixed Breeds" includes both pedigreed cats that are

not show quality due to some—often slight—deviation from the breed standard and cats whose ancestry is unknown. In the absence of a standard for the latter class, hopefuls are judged on traits including good looks and personality.

Information on showing your pedigreed cat or household pet can be obtained from magazines including *Cat Fancy* (*see page 245*), which publishes lists of upcoming shows every month, and from the following web sites, which provide details of their breed standards:

- American Cat Fanciers' Association (ACFA)
- Animal Network
- Cat Fanciers' Association (CFA)
- The International Cat Association (TICA)

Experienced breeders recommend that you find a mentor to introduce you to the show circuit. As Robin Dougherty explains in her article "The Road to Fame" *Cats USA*, 2001 Annual), "Showing a pedigreed cat takes perseverance—and a little help from friends."

In interviews with several breeders, Dougherty describes the experience of Tonkinese breeder Peggy Gyimesi at her first show: "the whirlwind of activity that first-time com

petitors and visitors discover. People, product booths and judging rings pack the room. There are hundreds of cats. The crowd surges through narrow aisles."

Breeder Jill Selkowitz of Tarkana, California, concurs. "You need to know how to find shows in your area, how to register and what to bring to the show": for example, cage curtains to keep your cat from becoming distracted, a litter box that fits into the cage, food and water dishes, and grooming tools. You also need information on how to act in the ring and on the fine points of scoring. For example, points are awarded for defeating other cats in various competition groups. The Best Cat in Show earns one point for each cat it defeats. The Championship class for unaltered (or "whole") pedigreed cats offers the title of champion to the cat which earns six winners' ribbons in this class. To become a grand champion, a cat must earn 200 points in CFA

competition. Premiership—the competition class for spayed or neutered pedigrees—also requires six winners' ribbons for the title of premier and 75 points in CFA competition for the title of Grand Premier. The Kittens class is for pedigreed cats older than four months and younger than eight months that are eligible for show. There is also an Exhibition class for cats and kittens entered by owners who want to display their animals at a show, but choose not to compete.

The U.S. show season runs from the first weekend in May to the last weekend of the following April, and new national and regional cat clubs are growing steadily in numbers and enthusiasm. However, breeders who show (or "campaign") are quick to assure newcomers that they are unlikely to make much money breeding cats. Birman breeder Paula Jo Watson (see pages 27–8), who owns Bitaheaven Cattery in Conway, Arkansas, with her husband James Watson, emphasizes that love of the breed, and of the cats, is their major motivation. "If you show and take the proper care of your animals, your veterinary bills and show expenses are going to far outweigh any profit you're going to make raising kittens." But the thrill of seeing your cat enjoy all the attention while collecting blue ribbons—or even the coveted brown ribbon—plus making a host of new friends in the fancy adds up to rewards that far outweigh the financial.

Major Cat Societies and Awards

Because show venues, member clubs, registration fees, and local news of the fancy change from year to year, the following major organizations are recommended as sources for up-to-date news of shows, standards, and other information you may need.

United States

Cat Fanciers' Association (CFA)
P.O. Box 1005
Manasquan, NJ 08736-0805
Tel: 732-528-9797
Fax: 732-528-7391

CFA Annual Awards Banquet, June
National Awards are presented to the highest-scoring ("Top") twenty-five Cats, twenty Kittens, and twenty (altered) Cats in Premiership. These National Winners are entitled to use the designation "NW" in their names. The Top Cats in the International Division are called Division Winners and use the designation "DW."

American Cat Fanciers' Association (ACFA)
P.O. Box 1949
Nixa, Missouri 65714-1949
Tel: 417-725-1530
Fax: 417-725-1533

ACFA Annual Awards Banquet, August
After completion of the show season (May 1-April 30), the scores of the cats in each class— Cat, Kitten, Alter, and Household Pet—are calculated, and each of the highest-scoring cats is designated "Best" in its class.

The International Cat Association (TICA)
P.O. Box 2684
Harlingen, Texas 78551
Tel: 956-428-8046
Fax: 956-428-8047

Canada

**Canadian Cat Association/
L'Association Feline Canadienne (CCA)**
289 Rutherford Road, S, #18
Brampton, Ontario L6W 3R9
Tel: 1 905-459-1481
Fax: 1 905-459-4023

All Canadian Awards Banquet, June
National awards are presented to the winners in five categories: Championship, Kittens, Premiership, Longhair, and Shorthair.

Europe

Governing Council of the Cat Fancy (GCCF)
4-6 Penel Orlieu
Bridgwater, Somerset
TA6 3PG, UK
Tel: +44 1278 427575

Cat Association of Britain
(The British member of the FIFe [Federation Internationale Feline], which spans thirty-seven countries)
Mill House,
Letcomb Regis, Oxon
OX12 9JD UK
Tel: +44 1235 766543

Plants Poisonous to Cats

Source: Dr. Jill Richardson, Veterinary Poison Information Specialist
American Society for the Prevention of Cruelty to Animals
National Animal Poison Control Center

A
Aloe Vera
Amaryllis

Apples (seeds)
Apple Leaf Croton
Apricot (pit)
Asparagus Fern
Autumn Crocus
Azalea

B
Baby's Breath
Bird of Paradise
Branching Ivy
Buckeye
Buddist Pine

C
Calla Lily

Castor Bean
Ceriman
Cherry
   (seeds/leaves)

Chinese Evergreen
Cineraria
Clematis
Cordatum
Corn Plant
Cornstalk Plant
Croton
Cuban Laurel
Cutleaf
   Philodendron
Cycads
Cyclamen

D
Daffodils
Devil's Ivy
Dieffenbachia
Dracaena Palm
Dragon Tree

E
Easter Lily

Elaine
Elephant Ears
Emerald Feather
English Ivy
Eucalyptus

F
Fiddle-leaf Fig
Florida Beauty
Foxglove
Fruit Salad Plant

G
Geranium

German Ivy
Giant Dumb Cane
Glacier Ivy
Gold Dust
   Dracaena
Golden Pothos

H
Hurricane Plant

I
Indian Rubber
   Plant

J
Janet Craig
   Dracaena
Japanese Show
   Lily
Jerusalem Cherry

K
Kalanchoe

L
Lily of the Valley

M
Marble Queen
Marijuana

Mexican
   Breadfruit
Miniature Croton
Mistletoe
Morning Glory

N
Narcissus
Needlepoint Ivy
Nephytis
Nightshade

O
Oleander

Onion
Oriental Lily

P
Peace Lily
Peach (pits/leaves)
Pencil Cactus
Plumosa Fern
Poinsettia

Poison Ivy

Poison Oak
Pothos
Precatory Bean
Primrose

R
Red Emerald
Red Princess
Rhododendron
Ribbon Plant

S
Sago Palm
Satin Pothos
Schefflera
Silver Pothos
String of Pearls
Sweetheart Ivy
Swiss Cheese
   Plant

T
Taro Vine
Tiger Lily
Tomato Plant
Tree
   Philodendron

W
Weeping Fig

Y
Yew

Helping Hands

United States

Alley Cat Allies
7920 Norfolk Avenue, Suit 600
Bethesda, MD 20814-2525

American Humane
(formerly American Humane Assoc.)
63 Inverness Drive East
Englewood, CO 80112-5117

American Society for the Prevention
of Cruelty to Animals (ASPCA)
424 East 92nd Street
New York, NY 10128

Assisi International Animal Institute, Inc.
P.O. Box 10166
Oakland, CA 94610-0166

Best Friends Animal Sanctuary
5001 Angel Canyon Road
Kanab, UT 84741-5001

The Company of Animals Fund (COAF)
C/o The Jefferson Center for Learning & the Arts
65 Jefferson Avenue
Columbus, OH 43215

The Fund for Animals
200 West 57th St.
New York, NY 10019

In Defense of Animals
3010 Kerner Blvd
San Rafael, CA 94901

Northeast Animal Shelter
204 Highland Avenue
Salem, MA 01970-0901
Tel: 978-745-9888

North Shore Animal League America
25 Davis Avenue
Port Washington, NY 11050

PetsMart Charities Adoption Centers
19601 N. 27th Avenue
Phoenix, AZ 85027

SpayUSA
c/o Pet Saver Foundation
2261 Broadbridge Ave.
Stratford, CT 06614

International

Royal Society for the Prevention of Cruelty to Animals - United Kingdom
Wilberforce Way
Southwater
Horsham
West Sussex, RH13 9RS

Royal Society for the Prevention of Cruelty to Animals - Australia
PO Box 265
Deakin West ACT 2600
Australia

Animal Rescue Network- Canada (Reseau Secours Animal)
PO Box 33203
St Andre Station
Montreal
QC H2L4Y5
Canada

Useful Books, Magazines, and Newsletters

Quarterly Newsletter
Association for Pet Loss and Bereavement
P.O. Box 106
Brooklyn, NY 11230

Beck, Ken, and Jim Clark. *The Encyclopedia of TV Pets: A Complete History of Television's Greatest Animal Stars.* Nashville, Tenn.: Rutledge Hill Press, 2002.

CAT FANCY magazine
P.O. Box 6050
Mission Viejo, CA 92690-6050
Monthly, & *CATS USA Annual*

Catnip: The Monthly Report for Caring Cat Owners
Tufts University School of Veterinary Medicine
Education Office:
  Catnip
  P.O. Box 2727
  Oceanside, CA 92501-2727

Cats & Kittens magazine
Pet Publishing Inc.
7-L Dundas Circle
Greensboro, NC 27407

CatWatch: The Newsletter for Cat People
Cornell University College of Veterinary Medicine
Education Office:
  CatWatch
  75 Holly Hill Lane
  Greenwich, CT 06830

Cawley, Janet. "Heroes: Michael Mountain of Best Friends Sanctuary," *Biography* magazine, February 2002.

Commings, Karen. *The Cat Lover's Survival Guide.* Hauppauge, N.Y.: Barron's Educational Series, 2001.

Fisher, Ann K. *Living in Shadows: How to Help the Stray Cat in Your Life (Without Adding to the Problem).* Los Angeles: Amythyst Publishing, 2002.

Fox, Michael W. *The Healing Touch: The Proven Massage Program for Cats and Dogs.* N.Y.: Newmarket Press, 1990.

Jankowski, Connie. *Adopting Cats and Kittens: A Care and Training Guide.* Howell Book House, 1993.

Johnson-Bennett, Pam. *Think Like a Cat: How to Raise a Well-Adjusted Cat, Not a Sour Puss.* N.Y.: Penguin, 2000.

Ludwig, Gerd. *My Dream Cat.* Hauppauge, N.Y.: Barron's Educational Series, 2001.

Masson, Jeffrey M. *The Nine Emotional Lives of Cats: A Journey into the Feline Heart.* N.Y.: Ballantine, 2002.

Thornton, Kim, illus. Keith Robinson. *Why Do Cats Do That?: Real Answers to the Curious Things Cats Do…with Training Tips.* Los Angeles: Bowtie Press, 2002.

Walker, Bob, and Frances Mooney. *The Cat's House.* N.Y.: Simon & Schuster/Andrews McMeel, 2001.

Wulff-Tilford, Mary L., and Gregory L. Tilford. *All You Ever Wanted to Know About Herbs for Pets.* Los Angeles: Bowtie Press, 2002.

Glossary

agouti Combination of light and dark banding along the length of individual hairs, notably in tabbies.

albino A cat with no color pigment at all, appearing pure white with pinkish eyes.

altered A cat that has had its reproductive organs removed (whether a spayed female or a neutered male).

awn hairs A coarser form of secondary hair, with thickened tips.

bib The part of the ruff, or long, thick hair, around the chest area

bicolor Coat showing areas of one solid color and patches of white.

blaze A marking, usually white, down the forehead and nose.

bloodline A group of cats related to each other through several generations, or by their pedigrees.

blue Blue-gray coloration.

breeches (Also called "britches") Long hairs on the back of the hind legs which run from the hips to the hock, or lower joint, of the leg.

breed Cats having a similar, defined appearance and related ancestry.

breed standard The criteria against which cats of particular breed/s are judged.

brush A profuse covering of hair on the tail, giving it a plumelike appearance, typical of long-haired cats.

calico A cat, usually female, having black and dark- and light-red markings on a coat that is more than half white. (Called Tortoiseshell and White in the UK).

cameo Hair with cream or red tipping, as seen on Chinchilla, shaded, or smoke coat patterns.

cat fancy The hobby of breeding, selling, and showing cats, usually pedigreed cats.

cat flap A door through which a cat can pass in and out; it may be lockable or standard.

cattery The place where a breeding cat is kept, either in the house or in a separate outbuilding.

champion Title accorded to a cat after a number of wins in shows.

chocolate Medium to pale brown; lighter than Seal in colorpoint cats.

cobby A sturdy, rounded, and compact body, usually set low on the legs, with broad shoulders and rump.

colorpoint A cat with darker shadings on its mask, ears, paws, and tail, e.g., the Siamese.

colostrum "First milk" of a mother cat, or queen, that has just given birth; provides vital antibody protection to the newborn kittens.

double coat A thick, longer topcoat over a short, soft undercoat; the skin is not visible when the coat is parted.

down hair Short, soft secondary hairs.

euthanasia To cause death in a painless and peaceful manner in order to end incurable illness and suffering. Also called "putting down."

feral cat An untamed domestic cat that was born in, or has reverted to, living on its own without human aid.

flanks The fleshy area between the cat's ribs and its hips.

gene Part of the chromosome from which hereditary traits are determined.

guard hairs Longer hairs forming topcoat.

hereditary Traits/genes passed down from parents to offspring.

in-breeding Mating together of cats that are closely related, e.g., male and female littermates.

in season The intermittent periods of time during which the female, or queen, is willing to mate with the male, or stud cat. Also called "in heat" and "estrus."

kink A twist, bend, curl, or bump in the tail bone.

laces White markings on the legs.

lavender Pale pinkish-gray coat coloration.

locket A white marking on the throat of a solid- or self-colored cat.

mackerel A type of tabby pattern in which the colors of the coat appear striped.

mittens White fur on forepaws, as seen in the Ragdoll breed.

mixed-breed A cat whose ancestry includes two or more different breeds that do not comprise a separate breed; not purebred. (Called a "moggy" in the UK.) Most household pets are random-bred, or mixed-breed, cats.

mutation A change in genes, whether accidental or environmental, giving rise to unexpected alterations in the appearance of kittens compared to that of parents.

muzzle The jaws and mouth.

neutered A cat that has been castrated (males) or spayed (females).

nose leather Area of skin on nose not covered by fur, often pink in color.

odd-eyed Having different colored eyes; usually one eye is blue and the other is yellow or copper.

Oriental The term used to describe lithe, fine-boned cats like the Siamese that have a foreign appearance.

outcross The pairing of one cat with another unrelated cat, possibly of a different breed.

outer coat Comprises the longer guard hairs.

pads The leathery areas without fur on the paws, corresponding to the toes.

purebred The result of deliberate pairings over a number of generations so as to produce the appearance and traits of previous generations.

quarantine A period of isolation to prevent the spread of disease. Different countries have their own regulations about the length of this period.

queen An unaltered female cat to be used for breeding purposes.

Persian Equivalent to Longhair in the UK.

recognition Acceptance of the standard for a new breed by a cat association.

ruff Longer, thicker hair around the neck and chest.

Rumpy A Manx cat with no trace of a tail.

stop A slight indentation at the bridge of the nose, between or just below the eyes.

stud cat An unaltered male cat used for breeding; also known as a tomcat.

tabby Coat markings that may be striped, blotched, spotted, or ticked (agouti).

tartar A brown, hardish deposit on the teeth that can lead to decay.

ticking Bands of color on individual hairs.

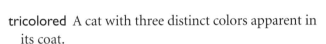

tortie Abbreviation for a tortoiseshell tabby (see below).

tortoiseshell A cat, usually female, showing black, and light- and dark-red areas in the coat.

tricolored A cat with three distinct colors apparent in its coat.

van pattern A coat mainly white, with color on the head and tail (e.g., the Turkish Van).

whisker pads The thickened or fatty pads around the whisker area.

Bibliography

Alderton, David. *Cats: Eyewitness Handbooks.* N.Y.: Dorling Kindersley, 1992

Beard, Henry. *Poetry for Cats: The Definitive Anthology of Distinguished Feline Verse.* N.Y.: Villard Books, 1994.

Berg, John, DVM, ed. *Catnip: The Monthly Report for Caring Cat Owners.* Medford, Mass.: Tufts University School of Medicine, 2002–03.

Bricklin, Mark. *Pets' Letters to God.* Emmaus, Pa.: Rodale Inc. for Hallmark Cards, 1999.

Caravan, Jill. *An Identification Guide to Cat Breeds.* N.Y.: Gallery Books, 1991.

Cole, Timothy H., ed. *CatWatch: The Newsletter for Cat People.* N.Y.: Cornell University School of Veterinary Medicine, 2001-03.

Dodman, Nicholas, DVM. *The Cat Who Cried for Help: Attitudes, Emotions and the Psychology of Cats.* N.Y.: Bantam Books, 1997.

Dratfield, Jim, and Paul Coughlin, Petography, Inc. *The Quotable Feline.* N.Y.: Alfred A. Knopf, 1996.

Jankowski, Connie. *Adopting Cats and Kittens: A Care & Training Guide.* N.Y: Howell Book House, 1993.

Johnson, Pam. *Cat Love: Understanding the Needs and Nature of Your Cat.* Pownal, Vt.: Storey Communications, 1990.

Luke, Amanda J. ed. *CATS USA: Annual Guide to Buying and Caring for Purebred Kittens.* Irvine, Calif.: Fancy Publications, 2001.

McGreevy, Paul, ed. *Cats: The Little Guides.* San Francisco: Fog City Press, 1999.

Morris, Desmond. *Cat World: A Feline Encyclopedia.* N.Y.: Penguin Books, 1997.

Papai, Franki B. *The Cat Lover's Cookbook.* N.Y.: St. Martin's Press, 1993.

Rothrock, Ellyce, ed. *CAT FANCY* magazine, Feb., June, and July 2002. Irvine, Calif.: Fancy Publications, 2002.

Rutherford, Alice P., ed. *The Reader's Digest Illustrated Book of Cats.* Montreal: The Reader's Digest Assoc., 1992.

Sommer, Robin Langley, ed. *The Little Book of Cats: Poems and Prose.* Rowayton, Conn.: DoveTail Books, in assoc. with Saraband Inc., 1999.

Siegal, Mordecai, ed. *Simon & Schuster's Guide to Cats.* N.Y.: Simon & Schuster, 1983.

Suares, J.C., ed., and Jane Martin. *Funny Cats.* N.Y.: Welcome Enterprises, 1995.

Thornton, Kim Campbell, and John Hamil, DVM. *Your Aging Cat: How to Keep Your Cat Physically and Mentally Healthy into Old Age.* N.Y.: Howell Book House, 1996.

My Cat's Record

Veterinarian:..
Address:...

....

....

Telephone:...
Emergency Clinic:...

....

....

Date	Immunization	Comments

Sick Visits:	Diagnosis	Treatment/Prescription

Photographer's Thanks

The photographer would like to thank the following for all their help in the making of this book: The Pet Centre, Dundalk, Co. Louth; Tracy Carlisle and ANCU Veterinary Hospital; Orlaith Hughes and Bunny; Naoimh Hughes and Claws; Roisin Hughes, Fearghal Hughes, and Maggie Murphy; Ronan and Aundrine Milton, Binny, Snowball, and Fred; Nick James and Ben; Charles Ziga and Hickory; The Cats of Dorsey; Chloe, Marc, and Lottie van Grieken, Fudge, and Squinky; The Bradley Family and Spike; Jane and Lydia Tarran, Jessie, Rosie, and Bramble; Iona and Cara Tavendale; Stephanie Swiatek; Heather and Rowan Howitt; John Francis McGivern, Richard, and Taff; Winifred and Max Robertson and Loismhor British Shorthaired Cats; Lynn and Ian Breslin and Hollygram Ragdolls; Jocelyn Montin; Michelle and Jade Beattie; Erwin deZwartes and Bemoedji Norwegian Forest Cats; Trudy Walsh and Ardbraccan Birmans; Carol Ervine, Vinny, and Gem; Claire Reeves and Sonny; C. & S. Caughey and Angel; John Cully, Maverick, and Purdy; Donna McWilliams and Clare; Lyn Orr, Mary Lo, and Blossom; Paul Sinta; Mr. And Mrs. M. Keenan, Shadow, and Tikka; and most importantly, Thelma.

Nick and Ben

Iona, Cara, and their fluffy friend

Heather, Rowan, and friends

Hickory

Chloe, Lottie, and Squinky

Orlaith and Claws, Naoimh and Spike

Lydia, Jessie, and Rosie

Honey and Jessie

Jade and Spike

Bunny

Fudge

Claws

INDEX

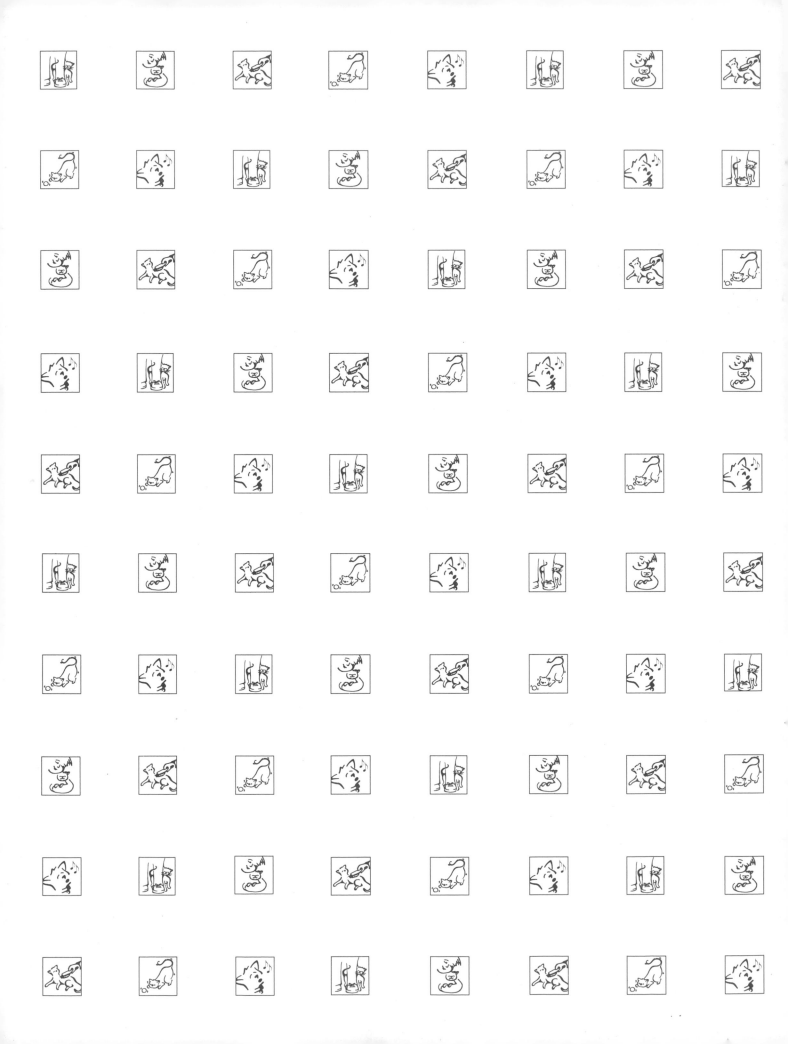